No one else
can match the effectiveness, the simplicity, or the appeal of the

SPECTRUM READING SERIES

Students gain meaningful practice—independently

With the SPECTRUM READING SERIES students not only get the practice they need in essential reading skills, they also enjoy being able to do it on their own.

In grades one through six, each lesson features an illustrated story followed by exercises in comprehension and basic reading skills. Because the same format is used consistently throughout, your students will have little trouble doing the lessons independently. And each two-page lesson can be finished easily in one class period.

Students develop and refine key reading skills.

- **Comprehension** exercises help students go beyond understanding of facts and details to drawing conclusions, predicting outcomes, identifying cause and effect, and developing other higher level comprehension skills.
- **Vocabulary development** builds on words from the reading selections. In addition to learning synonyms, antonyms, and words with multiple meanings, students develop sight vocabulary and learn to use context as a clue for meaning.
- **Decoding** exercises refine students' abilities to "attack" and understand new reading words.
- **Study skills** are developed by helping students apply their reading skills to new tasks, such as using reference materials, reading graphs, and applying other everyday life skills.

Reading selections captivate and motivate.

Students get their best reading practice by actually reading. That's why the selections in the SPECTRUM READING SERIES, in addition to offering practice in skills, also motivate students to read—just for fun.

Students quickly become friends with the characters in these entertaining stories. And they enjoy new levels of reading success—thanks in part to carefully controlled vocabulary and readability as well as beautiful illustrations.

The program adapts completely to any teaching situation.

The SPECTRUM READING SERIES can be used in many different ways.

- For the whole class . . . for intensive reinforcement of reading skills or to supplement a basal reading program.
- For reading groups . . . to provide skills practice at the appropriate levels.
- For individual use . . . to help build a completely individualized program.
- For at-home practice . . . to expand on skills learned in the classroom.

D1270649

SPECTRUM

Spectrum is an imprint of Frank Schaffer Publications.

Send all inquiries to: Frank Schaffer Publications • 3195 Wilson Drive NW • Grand Rapids, Michigan 49544

ISBN 1-56189-912-7   5 6 7 8 9 10 11 12 13 POH 09 08 07 06 05 04

Index of Skills for *Reading Grade 2*

Numerals indicate the exercise pages on which these skills appear.

Knowing the Words

Antonyms—89, 97, 103, 105, 111, 113, 127, 135, 139, 147

Classification—11, 27, 31, 55, 61, 65, 91, 101, 103, 109, 123, 125, 149

Multiple meanings—19, 39, 45, 51, 71, 83, 93, 99, 105, 115, 117, 119, 131, 137

Synonyms—95, 103, 107, 121, 129, 139, 151, 163

Word meaning from context—3, 7, 11, 19, 27, 31, 39, 45, 51, 55, 61, 65, 71, 83, 87, 89, 91, 93, 95, 97, 99, 101, 103, 109, 111, 113, 117, 119, 121, 123, 125, 133, 135, 137, 141, 153, 155, 165, 167

Working with Words

Base words and endings—15, 21, 69, 73, 85, 89, 133, 135, 151, 169

Blends—9, 21, 41, 69, 93, 97, 139, 165

Compound Words—47, 57, 67, 81, 107, 109, 123, 145, 159, 167

Consonant digraphs— 15, 47, 77, 81,107, 145, 163

Contractions—23, 43, 49, 75, 89, 99, 105, 117

Final consonants—5, 23, 29, 63, 87, 133, 143, 151

Initial consonants—5, 23, 29, 63, 87, 133, 143, 151

Irregular spellings—121, 123, 155

Long vowels—33, 37, 41, 57, 111, 129, 143

Possessives—25, 37, 53, 85, 97, 117, 141, 161, 167

Long vowels—33, 37, 41, 57, 111, 129, 143

Prefixes and suffixes—121, 143, 157, 163

r-Controlled vowels—43, 53, 59, 67, 139, 149, 153, 159

Rhyming words—29, 37, 53, 69, 101, 127, 147, 157

Short vowels—21, 25, 41, 59, 67, 73, 75, 77, 111, 129, 143, 47, 157, 161

Singular and plural—33, 49, 59, 73, 93, 105, 129, 149, 169

Syllables—115, 127, 155, 163

Variant sounds—63, 73, 77, 85, 153, 159, 161, 165

Vowel digraphs and diphthongs—43, 57, 63, 81, 125, 141, 145, 157, 163, 169

Reading and Thinking

Cause and effect—11, 17, 19, 21, 23, 63, 89, 91, 93, 97, 111, 117, 129, 131, 135, 149, 151, 153, 159, 167

Character analysis—93, 99, 115, 125, 133, 135, 139, 141

Comparison and contrast—97, 99, 103, 111, 123, 137, 157, 159

Context clues—5, 15, 29, 35, 37, 41, 43, 45, 53, 57, 59, 71, 73, 77, 79, 83, 95, 99, 101, 103, `05, 109, 115, 121, 125, 133, `35, 137, 139, 145, 147, 155, 157

Drawing conclusions—7, 9, 17, 21, 27, 31, 33, 37, 45, 47, 49, 51, 55, 65, 69, 75, 77, 79, 81, 83, 85, 89, 101, 107, 109, 117, 119, 123, 125, 129, 135, 137, 139, 145, 147, 155, 157

Facts and details—5, 7, 9, 13, 19, 23, 27, 31, 33, 35, 39, 47, 53, 55, 57, 61, 63, 65, 67, 71, 79, 81, 85, 87, 89, 91, 93, 97, 99, 107, 109, 117, 121, 123, 125, 135, 141, 149, 151, 153, 161, 163, 167

Main idea—3, 11, 19, 21, 25, 27, 31, 33, 35, 55, 59, 67, 87, 89, 91, 95, 109, 111, 113, 115, 119, 121, 125, 127, 1333, 141, 143, 147, 149, 151, 157, 159, 165, 167

Picture clues—23, 49, 61, 65, 73, 87, 139, 145, 157

Predicting outcomes—5, 11, 19, 51, 75, 83, 93, 97, 119, 129, 147, 151, 161, 167

Reality and fantasy—13, 15, 39, 41, 87, 91, 105, 107, 111, 123, 137, 159

Sequence—7, 17, 29, 45, 51, 55, 63, 81, 95, 103, 119, 129, 137, 145, 153, 155, 163, 169

Word referents—3, 25, 43, 69, 91, 101, 113, 127, 139, 143, 147

Learning to Study

Alphabetical order—13, 17, 35, 79, 91, 95, 113, 119, 131, 137

Following directions—*All activity pages*

SPECTRUM READING
Grade 2

Table of Contents

A Dog for Marta. 2
Marta Sees Nicky 4
Nicky Takes a Walk. 6
New Things for Nicky. 8
Too Much Barking. 10
A New Friend 12
Nicky Helps Mom 14
Splash! 16
Neighbors. 18
Nicky Runs Away 20
Nicky Comes Home. 22
The Kitten Stays 24
The Pet Doctor 26
A Rainy Day 28
A Lesson for Lee. 30
Get the Brush 32
Marta Writes a Letter. 34
Mail for Marta 36
Nicky Plays with Dad 38
Nicky Gets Wet. 40
Helping Others 42
Mike's New Airplane 44
A New Game?. 46
Bigfoot Learns to Sit. 48
Open the Door! 50
Pop, Pop, Pop! 52
A Close Call. 54
Better Than a Bath 56
Inky Gets the Milk 58
Keep Away 60
Marta Helps at Home 62
Bigfoot's Lesson 64
Plans for the Show. 66
Dad's Plans 68
Helping Friends. 70
The Signs Are Ready. 72
Good Places for Signs. 74
Beautiful Ribbons 76
Mom Helps the Show. 78
Nicky Remembers a Friend. 80
The Dog Show 82
Gold Ribbon Winner. 84
The Forest Story Teller 86
Thunder and Rain. 88
The Haircut. 90
The Tree Planter 92
The Skunks' Present 94
Make Way for Betsy. 96
A Narrow Escape 98
The String House 100
Breakfast with Barnie. 102
Seeing Double 104
Ruby Throat 106
Diver Hawk. 108
The Night Hunter 110
The Red Coats Are Coming. 112
Too Late for Supper 114
The Insect Eater 116
Whistler Digs a Home. 118
A Hard Day's Work 120
Chomper's Treasure 122
A Place to Hide. 124
Bumbles Finds a Friend. 126
A Road for Mice 128
Dropping In on Musky 130
Glenda Gives a Gift. 132
Molly Gets a Scare 134
The Shy Singer 136
Growing Up 138
Nibbler Makes a Mistake 140
The Shortcut. 142
Sunny to the Rescue. 144
A New Face at the Pond. 146
A Slip on a Slide 148
Lefty's Old Suit 150
Tony Takes a Dive. 152
Fooling Mrs. Buzz. 154
The Gold Coat. 156
Flash Firefly. 158
The Champion Jumper 160
Pokey Snail 162
Sam Saves the Day 164
Worms Don't Tell 166
A Well-Kept Secret 168
Answer Key 170

A Dog for Marta

Read about Marta's surprise.

1   Marta was eating breakfast slowly. She was in no hurry because she didn't have school that day. The telephone rang. Marta's mom answered, "Yes, we can come today. We'll be over later this morning."

2   She turned to Marta and said, "That was Aunt Rosa. She has a wonderful surprise for you."

3   "She has a surprise for me? What is it?" asked Marta.

4   Mom said, "Aunt Rosa found a dog, and she trained it for you."

5   "A dog! Great!" shouted Marta, jumping up and knocking over her chair. She ran to the closet for her coat and shoes. As she headed for the car, Marta called, "I'm ready to get my dog!"

Knowing the Words

Write the story words that have these meanings.

1. good or great

   _____
   (Par. 2)

2. place to keep coats

   _____
   (Par. 5)

3. went that way

   _____
   (Par. 5)

Reading and Thinking

1. This story is mostly about

   ____ Marta's chair.

   ____ Marta's surprise.

   ____ Marta's breakfast.

Words such as *he, she,* and *it* take the place of other words. Read these sentences. Then fill in the blanks.

   Marta shouted as she ran.

   She stands for *Marta*_____.

2. Her mom laughed as she talked.

   She stands for _____.

3. My dad talked as he worked.

   He stands for _____.

Marta Sees Nicky

What kind of dog does Marta get?

1 There stood Marta's dog! It was a little tan one with long hair and a short tail. The dog wiggled all over when it saw Marta.

2 "This dog likes me!" Marta said.

3 "Yes, she does," said Aunt Rosa. "I've been calling her Nicky."

4 "I like that name, Aunt Rosa. Come, Nicky," called Marta.

5 Right away, Marta felt a wet nose on her arm. She said, "Good girl, Nicky. I can see you are a well-trained dog."

6 "Here is the little book that helped me train her," Aunt Rosa said. "You may take it and her leash. Be sure to walk Nicky every day."

7 "I will, Aunt Rosa," Marta said. "I will take good care of her."

Reading and Thinking

Put each word in the right blank.

nose   hair   leash

1. She wiggled her _____.

2. My dog has a new _____.

3. Does Nicky have short _____?

Circle the right answer.

4. What will Marta do next?

    go to the library

    take Nicky home

    feed the birds

5. What helped Aunt Rosa train Nicky?

    _____

Working with Words

Circle the best word for each sentence.
Then write it in the blank.

1. Nicky _____ to Marta.

    can   ran   pan

2. Marta walked her _____.

    dog   does   did

3. Nicky wiggled her _____.

    eat   each   ear

Nicky Takes a Walk

Read to see why Marta likes walking with Nicky.

1   Marta and Nicky were walking in the park. Marta's friends were walking their dogs, too. Nicky trotted next to Marta. Marta was proud of her dog. She wanted everyone to see Nicky. She called, "Lee, come and see my dog!"

2   Lee headed their way, but her dog, Bigfoot, wanted to play in the park. Bigfoot pulled on the leash and ran the other way. Lee chased him and shouted, "Come back!"

3   Marta called to her other friends. "Christy and Joe, this is my dog! Come see her!" Christy's and Joe's dogs were not trained. They ran around a tree.

4   As she started to pet Nicky's side, Marta said, "What a good dog you are! Maybe you can show those other dogs how to take a walk."

Knowing the Words

Write the story words that have these meanings.

1. walked fast

_____
(Par. 1)

2. rope used to hold an animal

_____
(Par. 2)

3. ran after

_____
(Par. 2)

Reading and Thinking

1. What is the name of Lee's dog?

_____

Why do you think he is named that?

_____

_____

2. What happened first in the story? Put **1** by it. What happened next? Put **2** by it. Put **3** by the thing that happened last.

_____ Marta called to Christy and Joe.

_____ Marta saw Lee and her dog.

_____ Marta took Nicky to the park.

7

New Things for Nicky

Read to see what Marta buys.

1 Marta said, "Dad, could we buy Nicky one of those collars with a round tag? We need to put our name and telephone number on it."

2 "That is a good idea, Marta," her dad answered. "We'll go right after lunch."

3 Soon Marta, her dad, and Nicky were at the store. Marta found the tag and a collar she liked. Then the salesperson said, "Every dog should have its own dish."

4 Dad said to Marta, "Why don't we get two dishes? One will be for food, and one will be for water."

5 "Great idea, Dad," Marta said. She told the salesperson, "Two blue ones, please."

6 Marta's dad laughed, "I know you like blue best. Is it the color Nicky likes best, too?"

Reading and Thinking

1. What will Nicky's collar have on it?

_____

_____

2. Why did Marta buy two dishes?

_____

_____

3. Why did Marta pick a blue collar

and blue dishes? _____

_____

Working with Words

Circle the best word for each sentence.
Then write it in the blank.

1. The birds will _____ away.

        try   bright   fly

2. His hair is _____.

     break   black   drink

3. I am _____ you are here.

     flew   glad   blue

4. Who will win the _____?

     prize   place   grass

Too Much Barking

Read to see why Nicky barks so much.

1   One night after dinner, Marta's mom and dad sat in their chairs talking about Nicky. Her dad said, "Nicky is such a good dog. She is a real friend to Marta."

2   "You are right," Mom answered. "Nicky is a wonderful pet, but she does something I don't like. Every day when the mail comes, she barks. She should not bark so much."

3   "Can we stop her?" Dad asked. "Why does she do it, Marta?"

4   Marta said, "Nicky sees the mail carrier walk up to the house every day, but we never let her in. Nicky thinks that she is not a friend."

5   Marta's mom and dad were surprised. Her mom asked, "Why didn't I think of that?"

6   Dad said, "Now we need to think of a way to make her stop."

Knowing the Words

Write the story words that have these meanings.

1. someone you like a lot

   _____
   (Par. 1)

2. someone who can carry things

   _____
   (Par. 4)

Circle the three words in each line that belong together.

3. house   book   park   store
4. bark   fly   wiggle   jump
5. soup   lunch   dinner   breakfast
6. ball   friend   neighbor   aunt

Reading and Thinking

1. This story is mostly about
   _____ Nicky and the mail.
   _____ a bone for Nicky.
   _____ Mom's surprise.

2. Why does Nicky bark so much?

   _____

   _____

   _____

3. Can you think of a way to make Nicky stop barking?

   _____

   _____

11

A New Friend

What can be done to stop a barking dog?

1 The next day Marta met the mail carrier on the sidewalk. Then Marta and the carrier walked up to the house. Nicky watched, but she did not bark. Marta called, "Mom, have you met our mail carrier, Mrs. Smith?"

2 Mom walked outside and said, "I'm glad to know you, Mrs. Smith. May I get you a drink of water?"

3 Mrs. Smith said, "Yes, please."

4 "Do you like your work, Mrs. Smith?" Marta asked.

5 "Yes," she answered. "I like walking. I like talking to everyone, too."

6 Then Mrs. Smith looked at Nicky. She said softly, "Hello, girl."

7 Nicky's ears were back. She walked over and sniffed before she sat down quietly as if to say, "I'm glad you are my friend."

Reading and Thinking

Some of these sentences are about **real** things, things that could happen. Write **R** by them. The other sentences are about things that could not happen, **make-believe** things. Write **M** by them.

1. ____ A dog can run and play.

2. ____ A house can talk.

3. ____ A dog likes bones.

4. ____ A dog likes to read.

5. Why does Mrs. Smith like her job? _____

_____

Learning to Study

Write each set of words in A-B-C order.

1. mail   bark   know

_____

_____

_____

2. work   ears   please

_____

_____

_____

3. friend   carrier   drink

_____

_____

_____

Nicky Helps Mom

Read to see how Nicky's barking helps Marta's mom.

1   Mrs. Smith was gone, but Marta and her mom were still talking. Mom looked around and said, "We need to cut this grass today, Marta."

2   Then Nicky started to bark. She barked at Marta's mom and then ran back to the house. Mom said, "Oh, no, my bread! It will be burned!"

3   She ran into the kitchen and threw open the oven. There were the pans of bread. The bread was brown, but it was not burned. The family could still eat it.

4   Mom said, "Nicky, thank you for telling me the bread was done. When Marta called me, I walked out to see Mrs. Smith. I needed to hurry back in, but I didn't."

5   "Mom is right, Nicky. Sometimes barking is the right thing for a dog to do," Marta laughed as she petted Nicky.

Reading and Thinking

Put each word in the right blank.

started   petted   burned

1. He _____ to go away.

2. The wood _____ well.

3. We _____ the cat.

Write **R** by the sentences that are about **real** things. Write **M** by the sentences about **make-believe** things.

4. ____ Dogs can bake bread.

5. ____ People can bake bread.

6. ____ People bake bread in an oven.

7. ____ An oven keeps food cool.

Working with Words

A **base** word is a word without an ending. The words in each row have the same **base** word. Circle the ending of each one. Then write the **base** word in the blank.

1. calling   2. burning
   called   burned
   calls   burns

_____   _____

Circle the best word for each sentence. Then write it in the blank.

3. We'll eat _____ he comes.

   then   when   check

4. Please finish _____ apples.

   chase   those   shoes

Splash!

Where is it cool on a warm day?

1 Marta and Lee were tired from playing with their dogs. "Stop for a while!" shouted Lee. But Nicky and Bigfoot were not tired at all.

2 Then Marta said, "I've got an idea! It's cool at the creek. Why don't we go there to play?"

3 Lee said, "Great idea!" Soon they were heading for the creek. When they got there, Nicky sniffed the water where she saw little fish that could swim fast. All at once, Nicky jumped on one. Splash! When the water was quiet, Nicky looked for the fish. Where did it go?

4 Nicky didn't look for long. She soon found how much fun it was just to swim and splash. Marta laughed, "You look so funny when you are all wet, Nicky. Isn't it great to keep cool at the creek?"

Reading and Thinking

1. Marta and Lee went to the creek because _____ _____.

2. Why couldn't Nicky find any fish after she jumped in? _____ _____

3. Write **1, 2,** and **3** by these sentences to show what happened first, next, and last.

   ____ Nicky jumped into the water.

   ____ Lee said, "Stop for a while!"

   ____ Nicky sniffed the water.

Learning to Study

Write each set of words in A-B-C order.

1. tired   idea   creek

   _____

   _____

   _____

2. quiet   sniffed   fish

   _____

   _____

   _____

3. splash   cool   jumped

   _____

   _____

   _____

Neighbors

Do you think it's hard to make new friends? Does Marta?

1 "Get the ball, Nicky," said Marta. She threw it hard, and the ball flew high over the backyard fence. "Oh, no," said Marta. "Nicky, stay. I will get the ball."

2 Before Marta could move, a boy said, "Isn't this your ball?" He started to carry it to the fence.

3 "Yes, thanks," said Marta, as she took the ball. Marta threw it again for Nicky to chase.

4 The boy watched and said, "Does your dog know lots of tricks?"

5 Marta answered, "Yes, she does. I work with her a lot. You just moved here, didn't you?"

6 The boy nodded and said, "Yes, we moved here yesterday. My name is Mike. I have a collie, and his name is Flash. I would like him to know how to do tricks."

7 Marta said, "I'm Marta. This is Nicky. We want to be good neighbors. We can help you with Flash."

Knowing the Words

Write the story words that have these meanings.

1. run after

   _____
   (Par. 3)

2. moved the head up and down

   _____
   (Par. 6)

3. people who live near you

   _____
   (Par. 7)

Put a check by the meaning that fits the underlined word in each sentence.

4. Is it <u>hard</u> to make new friends?

   ____ something not soft

   ____ something not easy to do

5. I will <u>watch</u> Nicky play.

   ____ thing that tells time

   ____ look at

Reading and Thinking

1. What kind of dog is Flash?

   _____

2. This story is mostly about

   ____ Marta playing with Nicky.

   ____ a new neighbor.

   ____ Nicky's ball.

3. How will Nicky and Marta help

   Mike with his dog? _____

   _____

   _____

4. Flash can't do any tricks

   because _____

   _____.

Nicky Runs Away

Read to see why Nicky runs away.

1 "Here we are, Nicky," said Marta. "I will take off your leash. You can run, but stay in the park."

2 As soon as Marta said this, Nicky started to run down the street. She ran into a big car lot. Marta chased her, shouting, "Come, Nicky!"

3 Nicky was barking at four dogs that were barking, too. On top of a car, a little black cat with big eyes sat and shook. The dogs couldn't get to it, but the cat couldn't get away.

4 Nicky growled at one big dog, which turned and ran. The other dogs saw Marta and ran, too.

5 Then Nicky sat next to the car and waited. Marta walked up and gave Nicky a big smile. "Good dog, Nicky. You chased away those mean dogs," she said as she helped the little cat down.

Reading and Thinking

1. This story is mostly about

   ____ Nicky playing.

   ____ Nicky finding a kitten.

   ____ Nicky holding a kitten.

2. The four dogs were barking

   because _____

   _____.

3. What makes you think that

   Nicky likes kittens? _____

   _____

   _____

Working with Words

Circle the best word for each sentence. Then write it in the blank.

1. This _____ likes me.

   cat   call   cut

2. I will _____ a drink.

   gave   got   get

Write **-ing** or **-ed** in each blank.

3. I talk _____ with her yesterday.

4. She want _____ to work.

5. Now she is help _____ us.

Circle the right word for each sentence. Then write it in the blank.

6. Mike is my best _____.

   ground   proud   friend

7. I need a _____ of water.

   trick   drink   break

Nicky Comes Home

What does Nicky bring home?

1 Marta's dad had dinner almost ready. Did he hear a noise outside? When he looked, he saw Nicky with a furry black thing in her mouth. "Nicky, what do you have there?" asked Dad.

2 Nicky walked in and set the thing on the floor. It wiggled and made a little noise. When it stood up, Marta's dad saw that it was a wet kitten. He picked it up as Marta's mom walked into the room.

3 "It isn't hurt, just very wet," Dad told her.

4 Mom said, "It's so little that I think it still needs a mother. Nicky, will this be your own pet cat?" Nicky's tail pounded the floor.

5 Then Marta ran into the room. She had been listening as her mom and dad talked. Marta said, "I knew you would let it stay!"

Reading and Thinking

Look at each picture and circle the sentence that goes with it.

1. Nicky is playing outside.

   Nicky is playing in the house.

2. Nicky sleeps on Marta's bed.

   Nicky sleeps in her basket.

3. Who fixed dinner? _____

4. How did Nicky carry the kitten?

   _____

5. Why did Marta stay outside?

   _____

Working with Words

Circle the best word for each sentence. Then write it in the blank.

1. Nicky's collar has a _____.

   tag   than   tail

2. Nicky can be a _____ dog.

   get   quiet   paint

3. The little kitten was _____.

   pet   met   wet

Write these sentences. Use one of the shorter words from the box to stand for the words that are underlined.

| we'll   isn't   can't   didn't   I'm |

4. We will be there.

   _____

5. He did not go.

   _____

6. The kitten is not hurt.

   _____

7. I am hungry.

   _____

8. Flash cannot do tricks.

   _____

The Kitten Stays

Read to see whom the kitten likes best.

1   Marta's dad was still holding the little kitten. "We need to talk, Marta. Does this kitten belong to anyone?"

2   Marta answered, "I don't think so. Nicky and I found it at the car lot. Please, may we keep it?"

3   "Tomorrow," said Dad, "you should go back there and tell them our telephone number. If no one calls for the kitten, you may keep it."

4   "Good idea," said Marta's mom. "For now, warm some milk for this hungry kitten. I will make a bed."

5   Marta's mother found a little box and lined it with a soft blanket. "The kitten should like this bed," she said. "It's just right for him."

6   But the kitten had ideas of his own. When Marta's mom looked into the room that night, he was in Nicky's basket. The kitten was sleeping between Nicky's paws.

Reading and Thinking

1. This story is mostly about

    ____ warming the milk.

    ____ talking about dogs.

    ____ the kitten's new home.

Fill in the blanks.

2. Mom said, "Good idea," as she warmed the milk.

    She stands for _____.

3. Mom found a box and lined it with a blanket.

    It stands for _____.

Working with Words

Circle the best word for each sentence. Then write it in the blank.

1. The milk is too _____.

    hit   hot   hat

2. The kitten's eyes are _____.

    big   bag   buy

3. Marta's mom made a _____.

    back   bed   bird

4. They have a _____ pet.

    now   not   new

Read these words and look at the pictures.

Marta's mom   her mom's hand

You can see that you add *'s* when you want to show that the hand belongs to Mom. Now write these names the same way.

5. Marta _____ hand

6. Mike _____ hand

The Pet Doctor

Why does Marta take her pet to the doctor?

1   Nicky, Marta, and the kitten were playing ball. Marta's dad walked into the room. "Marta, it looks as if you have fun with your pets," he said.

2   "I do, Dad. Nicky and I really like this kitten. We call him Inky."

3   "That is a good name for a black cat," her dad laughed. "Marta, we need to take Nicky and Inky to the doctor. We want them to stay healthy." Soon Marta, Dad, Nicky, and Inky were heading for the pet doctor.

4   A woman showed them to a little room, and the doctor came in to check Nicky and Inky. Her hands felt their soft coats. She looked into their eyes, ears, and mouths. Then she said, "I can tell that you take good care of your pets. Keep up the good work!"

5   Marta said, "I will do my best to keep them healthy."

Knowing the Words

Write the story words that have these meanings.

1. someone who keeps you well

_____
(Par. 3)

2. to be well

_____
(Par. 3)

3. to look over with care

_____
(Par. 4)

Circle the three words in each line that belong together.

4. arms   flowers   feet   hands

5. eyes   ears   doctor   mouth

6. hair   brown   white   black

Reading and Thinking

1. This story is mostly about

___ pets who are not well.

___ a mean doctor.

___ keeping pets healthy.

2. What four things did the doctor check on Nicky and Inky?

_____

_____

_____

_____

3. What do you think Marta can do to keep her pets healthy?

_____

_____

A Rainy Day

What can happen on a rainy day?

1 "Why did it have to rain?" said Marta. "Today we were going to start the dog-training lessons. Now there is nothing to do."

2 Then there was a knock on the door. Nicky barked and ran over to it. The knock sounded again, and Nicky pounded her tail on the floor. Slowly Marta walked to the door.

3 There stood her friends Lee, Joe, Christy, and Mike with a boy Marta didn't know. Mike said, "Marta, this is my friend Allen. He just got a new puppy."

4 Joe said, "We need lessons in dog training just as much as our dogs do. It was raining too much to work outside. We thought we could learn a lot working here with Nicky."

5 Nicky barked and wiggled all around. Marta said, "Come in, everyone. We won't let a little rain stop us, will we?"

Reading and Thinking

Put each word in the right blank.

puppy   learn   door

1. Please open the _____.

2. Children _____ at school.

3. My _____ has black eyes.

4. Write **1, 2,** and **3** by these sentences to show what happened first, next, and last.

_____ Marta was glad to see her friends.

_____ Nicky barked and ran to the door.

_____ There was a knock on the door.

Working with Words

Circle the best word for each sentence. Then write it in the blank.

1. Can you read this _____?
   cook   look   book

2. Marta _____ Allen today.
   mail   met   mean

3. Nicky pounded her _____ on the floor.
   tail   fill   well

The missing word in each sentence sounds like *right*. Change the *r* in *right* to *f*, *l*, or *n*. Write the new words. The first one is done.

4. *fight* _____ _____

Use the words you made in sentences.

5. Please turn off the _____.

6. We will not _____ over the toys.

7. It rained last _____.

A Lesson for Lee

Is it easy to train a dog?

1 Marta started with an easy lesson. She said, "First, your dog needs to know its name. When it comes, pet it a lot like this." Then Marta called, "Nicky, come!" When Nicky did, Marta petted her and said, "Good dog!"

2 Everyone but Lee thought it was a good trick. She said, "That is easy!"

3 Marta said, "Now you try it."

4 Lee called loudly, "Here, Nicky," but Nicky did not move at all.

5 Marta said, "She knows only one word for every trick. Say *come.*"

6 Lee said, "Well, I will try it. Nicky, come." Nicky trotted right over to Lee, and Lee said in surprise, "She did it!"

7 Marta didn't smile but said, "You have to show her you are glad she did it. That is important."

8 Lee petted Nicky on the head and said, "Oh, Nicky, you good dog!"

9 Marta laughed and asked, "Lee, will it be as easy to train your dog as it was to train you?"

Knowing the Words

Write the story words that have these meanings.

1. not hard

   _____
   (Par. 1)

2. what you call someone

   _____
   (Par. 1)

Circle the three words in each line that belong together.

3. walk   look   trot   run
4. head   tail   trick   feet
5. good   mean   great   wonderful

Reading and Thinking

1. This story is mostly about

   ____ how to pet your dog.

   ____ a meeting at Marta's.

   ____ Mike's dog.

2. What did Marta say a dog must know first?

   _____

3. Tell one important lesson that

   Lee learned. _____

   _____

   _____

4. Why do you think a dog learns faster if you say "good dog"?

   _____

   _____

   _____

Get the Brush

What did Marta forget to do?

1 Marta's dad said, "Marta, I'm glad that you walk Nicky so much, but you need to brush her more. She looks like a string mop."

2 Marta looked at her dog. Nicky's hair did need brushing. She said, "You are right, Dad, and I will brush her now." Off Marta ran to get the brush.

3 Soon she was outside brushing Nicky. When she saw Mike in his yard with Flash, she called, "Come on over. We'll brush our dogs."

4 They worked with care for a long time. When Mike was done, he said, "Flash, you are beautiful." Then he asked, "Marta, do you have a bag for all this hair?"

5 Marta said, "Don't throw away that hair, Mike. Birds like to use it in their nests. I put Nicky's hair by the bird feeder."

6 Marta looked down at her dog and said, "Now you look great, Nicky! I'm going to brush you every day. We will help the birds a lot."

Reading and Thinking

1. This story is mostly about

　　____ brushing dogs.

　　____ brushing Marta's hair.

　　____ Marta's dad.

2. Marta's dad said Nicky looked

　　like a _____.

3. Why should you talk quietly
and pet your dog when you
brush it?

_____

_____

_____

Working with Words

Circle the best word for each
sentence. Then write it in the
blank.

1. Birds like to _____ hair
in their nests.

　　　　us　　　up　　　use

2. I can _____ bread.
　　　back　　　bake　　　book

3. I _____ to brush my dog.
　　　little　　　like　　　let

Read these words and look at the
pictures.

　　　cat　　　　　　　cats

You can see that you add *s* to
show that you mean more than one
cat. Write these words so that
they mean more than one.

4. dog _____

5. bird _____

6. ear _____

Marta Writes a Letter

What did Marta say in her letter?

Dear Grandmother and
Grandfather,

1   I want to tell you about my new
dog, Nicky. She is wonderful.
Aunt Rosa trained Nicky to do lots
of tricks. Now Nicky and I are
training my friends' dogs to come,
sit, and stay. I've been working on
a special trick with Nicky. I won't
even tell you what it is until she's
got it just right.

2   I try to take good care of Nicky.
When she needs it, I give her a
bath. She loves to splash!

3   Nicky has her own pet, a kitten
named Inky. She found Inky at the
car lot. Now Inky likes Nicky best
of all and sleeps in Nicky's basket.

4   Nicky is sniffing this letter. I
think she knows it is about her.

5   Soon we will have a dog show
in the park. Please try to come.

Love,
Marta

34

Reading and Thinking

Put each word in the right blank.

    special   bath   letter

1. Why is today so _____?

2. Nicky likes her _____.

3. Marta wrote a _____.

4. Who trained Nicky to sit?

    _____

5. What is going to happen soon?

    _____

6. This letter is mostly about
    ____ Marta and her friends.
    ____ the special trick.
    ____ Nicky.

Learning to Study

Write each set of words in A-B-C order.

1. trained   bath   special

    _____

    _____

    _____

2. care   splash   trick

    _____

    _____

    _____

3. pet   basket   sleeps

    _____

    _____

    _____

Mail for Marta

Who sent a letter to Marta?

Dear Marta,

¹ Thank you for your letter. It came in today's mail, and we were delighted to hear from you.

² We would love to come to your dog show. It will be a lot of work for you to put on a show. Are your friends going to help? Will you surprise everyone with that special trick then?

³ It's good that you know how to give Nicky a bath. That way you can always keep her clean.

⁴ When your mother was a girl, she had a dog, too. That dog used to hide your mother's things. Does Nicky hide your things?

⁵ We can't wait to see Nicky's pet kitten. Does Inky still like Nicky best? Nicky and Inky seem to be special friends.

⁶ We'll be seeing you soon.

Love,
Grandmother
and Grandfather

Reading and Thinking

Put each word in the right blank.

hide   clean   delighted

1. My hands are _____.

2. I am _____ to see you.

3. Will Nicky _____ this bone from me?

4. Why do you think that Marta's grandmother and grandfather like dogs? _____

_____

Working with Words

Circle the best word for each sentence. Then write it in the blank.

1. Nicky has a cold _____.

   nose   not   now

2. We will _____ a walk.

   talk   take   tail

The missing word in each sentence sounds like *make*. Change the *m* in *make* to *b, t,* or *w*. Write the new words.

3. _____ _____ _____

Use the words you made in sentences.

4. May we _____ a walk?

5. I like to _____ bread.

6. Did Nicky _____ you?

You know that *Mom's hand* means "the hand of Mom." Add *'s* when you write these names to show what belongs to each.

7. Dad _____ coat

8. Mike _____ book

9. Nicky _____ teeth

37

Nicky Plays with Dad

Read to see what game Nicky and Dad are playing.

1   Every morning Marta, her mom, and her dad worked around the house. Each one always did the same job.

2   Marta cleaned up the breakfast dishes. Inky stayed with Marta to help clean up any milk. Marta's mom worked in the garden while the day was still cool. Her dad made the beds, and Nicky would try to help.

3   To make a bed, Marta's dad pulled the blankets from one side and then the other. One day when he shook the top blanket, the end of it brushed Nicky's nose.

4   Nicky liked that—a new game! Dad was playing with her! Nicky jumped up and pulled on the blanket with her mouth. Dad shouted, "Let go, Nicky! Give me that blanket."

5   Playing with Marta's dad was so much fun. Nicky shook the blanket and growled.

6   Dad picked up a newspaper and hit the floor with it. This time Nicky let the blanket go. She did not like that noise. She understood that Marta's dad was not playing.

Knowing the Words

Write the story words that have these meanings.

1. work you do

   _____
   (Par. 1)

2. made a low sound

   _____
   (Par. 5)

Put a check by the meaning that fits the underlined word in each sentence.

3. The blanket will <u>brush</u> Nicky's nose.

   ____ thing used to fix hair

   ____ move over softly

4. Will Dad <u>play</u> with Nicky?

   ____ have fun

   ____ a show

Reading and Thinking

1. Who cleaned up after breakfast? _____

2. How did Inky help? _____

   _____

Write **R** by the sentences that are **real** things. Write **M** by the sentences that are about **make-believe** things.

3. ____ People can make beds.

4. ____ Dogs can make beds.

5. ____ Cats can weed flowers.

6. ____ People can weed flowers.

Knowing the Words: Word meaning from context (1–2); Multiple meanings (3–4). **Reading and Thinking:** Facts and details (1–2); Reality and fantasy (3–6).

39

Nicky Gets Wet

What is Nicky's surprise?

1   At last Marta had the sidewalk clean, so she put the broom away. Marta's mom was done weeding the flowers, too.

2   "Now we must water the grass," said Mom. "The ground is dry, and the grass needs water."

3   Marta helped her mother put the watering hose in the yard. Then they walked up to the house to turn on the water.

4   "Come, Nicky!" Marta shouted. "You had better stand back."

5   But Nicky wanted to see what was on the grass. She sniffed the hose. What was this funny thing in the yard? How still it was!

6   The thing started to get big. When it was big enough, it sent water up in little streams. Water went all over the grass, and all over Nicky, too.

7   Nicky jumped back. She liked most surprises, but not this one. She opened her mouth to bark, and water flew into it. Wet, wet Nicky! There was water on her and water in her!

Reading and Thinking

Put each word in the right blank.

streams   hose   dry

1. We use a _____ to water our flowers.

2. _____ of water ran down the window.

3. Is the paint _____?

Write **R** by the sentences that are about **real** things. Write **M** by the sentences about **make-believe** things.

4. _____ A yard can walk.

5. _____ A dog can walk.

6. _____ Birds can fly.

7. _____ Dogs can fly.

Working with Words

Circle the best word for each sentence. Then write it in the blank.

1. She likes to _____ flowers.

    pet   pan   pick

2. Sit _____ and read.

    back   bake   best

3. I like _____ book.

    think ·   thank   that

Fill in the missing vowel (*i, o,* or *u*) so the sentence makes sense.

4. Write on the l___ne.

5. Please give Nicky a b___ne.

6. May Nicky ___se this pan?

Fill in each blank with **str** or **spr** so the sentence makes sense.

7. Here is a ball of _____ing.

8. I will _____ay the grass.

9. Don't walk in the _____eet.

Helping Others

Why will Marta ride her bicycle today?

1 One day Mike's mother called Marta on the telephone. She said, "Marta, I need some things from the store. Mike can't go now. Could you get the things for me?"

2 "I will ask my mom," Marta said.

3 Her mother said yes, so Marta rode over to Mike's house on her bicycle. Nicky walked with her. Mike's mother gave Marta some money. "Marta," she said, "my things won't cost this much. You may spend what is left."

4 At the store, Marta found the things for Mike's mother. Then she picked out a good bone for Nicky. She was looking at things for herself when she saw a red ball. Nicky had one, but Flash didn't. She got the ball for Flash. On the way home, the ball fell out of Marta's bag. She looked back to see where it was. Then she saw Nicky carrying Flash's ball.

5 Marta was glad to be helping her neighbors. Nicky was helping, too.

Reading and Thinking

Put each word in the right blank.

cost   spend   bicycle

1. I have a new _____.

2. I will _____ my own money.

3. Does this ball _____ much?

Fill in the blanks.

4. Flash's ball fell so Nicky carried it.

   It stands for _____.

5. Marta and Nicky were happy because they were helping.

   They stands for _____

   and _____.

6. Nicky was carrying the ball as she ran.

   She stands for _____.

Working with Words

Circle the best word for each sentence. Then write it in the blank.

1. Did Marta _____ Nicky?

   day   tail   train

2. Can you _____ Nicky bark?

   heel   hear   head

3. Put on your warm _____.

   coat   cook   clean

Change each underlined word to two words. Write them on the line.

4. Flash <u>didn't</u> have a ball.

   _____

5. This <u>isn't</u> my bicycle.

   _____

Circle the right letters for each sentence. Then write them in the blank.

6. I st_____ted to sit up.

   er   ar   ir

7. This book is too sh_____t.

   or   er   at

8. Did the salesp_____son help?

   or   er   ar

Mike's New Airplane

Read to see what happened to Mike's airplane.

1 One day Marta and Mike went to the toy store. Mike wanted something special. The salesperson showed them many toys. When they left the store, Mike owned an airplane that would really fly. He was proud of his new toy. He wanted to take good care of it.

2 Later Mike and Marta walked to the park to try the airplane. They took Flash and Nicky with them. Mike threw the airplane first. It floated over some evergreens and landed at his feet.

3 "See how easy it is, Marta. It is fun to watch. Now you try."

4 Marta threw the airplane, but she did not fly it right. The airplane floated for just a short time. Then it fell and hit Nicky! Nicky jumped up and barked at it. Then she picked it up and shook it.

5 Mike's new airplane couldn't be fixed! It would not fly again. Marta said, "Mike, I will buy you another airplane, and we won't let Nicky near it."

Knowing the Words

Write the story words that have these meanings.

1. moved on the air

_____
(Par. 2)

2. trees with leaves that stay green

_____
(Par. 2)

3. came to the ground

_____
(Par. 2)

Put a check by the meaning that fits the underlined word in the sentence.

4. Did Marta know how to throw the airplane <u>right</u>?

_____ not on the left

_____ not the wrong way

Reading and Thinking

Put each word in the right blank.

owned   proud   evergreens

1. I am _____ of my dog.

2. We planted _____ in our yard.

3. Mike _____ a new toy.

4. Write **1, 2,** and **3** by these sentences to show what happened first, next, and last.

_____ Nicky shook Mike's toy.

_____ Mike got an airplane.

_____ Marta said that she would buy another airplane.

5. Why does Marta want to buy Mike a new airplane?

_____

_____

45

A New Game?

What is Nicky's new game?

¹ One day Marta's mother was pulling weeds in the flower bed, and Marta wanted to help. "That looks like fun. May I do that, too?"

² "No," Mom said. "You may not know which ones are going to be flowers and which ones are weeds. Sometimes it's hard to tell. If you want to help, you can sweep the sidewalk for me. Will you do that?"

³ "Sure, Mom," said Marta. She got the broom and started to sweep. Nicky ran to Marta because sweeping looked like a new game.

⁴ "Get out of the way, Nicky," said Marta. "You are standing right where I want to sweep." But Nicky thought Marta wanted to play. She did not understand. Every time the broom moved near her, Nicky jumped at it. At last Marta shouted, "Nicky, I'm trying to help Mom. Now stop!" She shook the broom at Nicky.

⁵ This time Nicky understood. Marta was not playing a new game.

Reading and Thinking

1. When you are weeding, why do you have to know the flowers from the weeds?

   _____

   _____

2. Why did Nicky try to jump on the broom? _____

   _____

3. What did Marta do to make Nicky understand she was not playing a game? _____

   _____

Working with Words

Read each sentence and circle the word that is made of two shorter words. Write the two words on the lines.

1. You can sweep the sidewalk.

   _____ _____

2. Nicky did not understand.

   _____ _____

3. Will someone please help?

   _____ _____

Circle the best word for each sentence. Then write it in the blank.

4. Please _____ us a trick.
   who   show   those

5. Where are your _____?
   this   who's   shoes

6. Nicky will _____ me.
   shook   chase   shout

Bigfoot Learns to Sit

How does Marta train Bigfoot to sit?

1   "For the last time, Bigfoot, sit!" said Lee, but Bigfoot lay down again. "Oh, you mean dog!"

2   Marta laughed, "He just does not understand when you say *sit*. What can we try that will work?"

3   Just then Lee's mother came out of the house and set down a dish of hot dogs. "Have a good lunch," she said. Lee started to get a hot dog.

4   "Wait, Lee," said Marta. Then, holding up a hot dog, she said, "Sit, Bigfoot." When Bigfoot started to stand up to get it, Lee pushed down on the dog's back end. Not meaning to, Bigfoot sat up.

5   "Good boy, Bigfoot!" said Marta. She gave him that hot dog and started to get another one. This time Bigfoot knew what to do.

6   Later, Lee went in to ask for more food. "You hungry children," said Lee's mother. Then she looked at Bigfoot, who did not seem hungry. "I can see who had a good lunch," she laughed.

Reading and Thinking

Look at each picture and circle the sentence that goes with it.

1. Nicky likes the water.

   Nicky does not like the water.

2. A mother can work.

   A mother can read.

3. He loves Bigfoot.

   He doesn't like Bigfoot.

4. Where are the children working with Bigfoot?

   _____

   How do you know? _____

   _____

Working with Words

Write these sentences. Use one shorter word for the two words that are underlined.

1. She <u>does not</u> know my name.

   _____

   _____

2. Bigfoot <u>will not</u> sit.

   _____

   _____

3. <u>It is</u> a beautiful day.

   _____

   _____

4. <u>I am</u> glad today.

   _____

Write these words so that they mean more than one. One is done for you.

house _____*houses*_____

5. mother _____

6. dog _____

7. boy _____

Open the Door!

What is Nicky's new trick?

1 It was a rainy day. Mom and Dad were watching television. Inky was sleeping. Marta and her friends were working on plans for their dog show. Nicky was playing in the kitchen. She would hit a ball with her paws and then run after it.

2 Marta's dad looked up from the television. He saw that it was raining hard now. He thought, "I must check to see if the newspaper is here. It's time for the carrier to come." Dad got up from his chair and walked outside, but he didn't shut the door.

3 Just then Nicky's ball hit the door. Nicky ran after the ball and hit the door, too. The door shut.

4 Dad could not get into the house. It was raining hard, and he was wet. "Open the door," he called.

5 Marta ran to open it and said, "Look, Dad. Nicky knows a new trick! She can shut the door."

6 "Yes, I know," laughed her dad. "But why did she have to learn it when I was outside on a rainy day?"

Knowing the Words

Write the story words that have these meanings.

1. thing that shows pictures

_____
(Par. 1)

2. ideas or ways of doing

something _____
(Par. 1)

3. room used for cooking

_____
(Par. 1)

Put a check by the meaning that fits the underlined word in each sentence.

4. Nicky <u>can</u> shut the door.

____ a thing to hold food

____ knows how to

5. I must <u>check</u> for the newspaper.

____ make a line

____ look with care

Reading and Thinking

1. Why do you think Marta's dad didn't open the door himself?

_____

_____

2. Do you think Nicky will shut the

door again? _____

Why or why not? _____

_____

_____

3. Write **1, 2,** and **3** by these sentences to show what happened first, next, and last.

____ Marta's dad looked for the newspaper.

____ Marta's dad watched television.

____ Marta saw Nicky's new trick.

51

Pop, Pop, Pop!

What can you do on a slow day?

1 Marta and her friends stood at the door of Mom's room. When Marta knocked, her mother said, "Yes?"

2 "What can we do?" asked Marta. "Tell us something new to do."

3 Mom said, "It's always fun to pop popcorn. Would you like to do that?"

4 "Oh, yes," answered the children. Mom told them what to do and watched as they worked. Soon the popcorn started to pop. Pop, pop, pop! A wonderful smell filled the kitchen.

5 Inky had been sleeping on top of the television. Now she jumped and landed on Nicky, who was sleeping on the floor. The kitten started to play with Nicky's paws. Nicky barked and wiggled. Everyone laughed, and Marta said, "The popping noise didn't wake Nicky, but Inky did!"

6 At last the popcorn was quiet. When Marta opened the top of the pan to look in, a piece jumped up and hit Nicky.

7 "Shut the top!" said Joe.

8 "You do it! I need to pet my poor dog!" laughed Marta.

Reading and Thinking

1. Why did Nicky wake up?

_____

_____

Put each word in the right blank.

wonderful   wake   piece

2. Warm bread smells

_____.

3. Please give me a _____ of bread.

4. Will you _____ me?

Working with Words

The missing word in each sentence sounds like *stop*. Change the *st* in *stop* to *t, m,* or *p.* Write the new words and put them in the right sentences.

1. _____ _____ _____

2. Some popcorn didn't _____.

3. I hit the _____ of my head.

4. Clean the floor with a _____.

Circle the right letters for each sentence. Then write them in the blank.

5. They walked in the p_____k.

     er   ir   ar

6. What happened f_____st?

     ar   or   ir

Add *'s* to these words to show what belongs to each one.

7. dog   the _____ collar

8. cat   the _____ head

9. bird   the _____ nest

10. kitten   the _____ ball

A Close Call

Read to see what happened to Flash.

1 Marta and Nicky were playing in the yard. All at once Marta saw Flash, Mike's dog, playing in the muddy park. She didn't see Mike at all. "That's funny," thought Marta. "Mike never lets Flash out alone." Flash was walking in the street when Marta saw a fast car.

2 Still no Mike! As loudly as she could, Marta shouted, "Flash, come!"

3 Right away, Flash ran to Marta. Flash was so glad to see her!

4 Marta threw her arms around him and said, "That was a close call. You almost got hurt, Flash. I'm glad Mike has been training you to come when he calls your name."

5 Marta was delighted that the dog lessons had helped Flash. As she petted him, Flash jumped up. Now Marta was muddy, too!

6 "We must hurry home," Marta told Nicky. "I've got to call Mike. I need to tell him that I found Flash and that we really need a bath!"

Knowing the Words

Write the story words that have these meanings.

1. near

   _____
   (Par. 4)

2. so glad

   _____
   (Par. 5)

Circle the three words in each line that belong together.

3. paws   tail   soft   head
4. glad   delighted   pleased   sad
5. paint   grass   park   yard

Reading and Thinking

1. This story is mostly about

   ____ a fast car.

   ____ Mike's bicycle.

   ____ Marta helping Flash.

2. Why was Flash walking in the

   street by himself? _____

   _____.

3. How had the dog lessons

   helped Flash? _____

   _____

4. Write **1, 2,** and **3** to show what happened first, next, and last.

   ____ Flash ran to Marta.

   ____ Marta called to Flash.

   ____ Marta played in her yard.

Better Than a Bath

Read to see what is better than a bath.

1 Marta put the two dogs in the backyard. Then she headed inside to call Mike and to wash off the mud.

2 Her dad met her at the back door and said, "Oh, no, you don't! Our house is clean right now, so you need to use the hose to wash off. This mud needs to stay outside where it belongs!" Then he shut the door.

3 Marta knocked on the door. When her dad opened it again, Marta said, "If I can't come in, will you call Mike and then hold the telephone for me so I can talk?" Soon she was saying, "Hello, Mike? Flash is here in my backyard."

4 Mike said, "You found him! Good!"

5 Marta went on, "Yes, now go and put on your swimsuit because you and I can wash our dogs with the hose. Flash and I are too muddy to take a bath inside."

6 Mike said, "All right. I will be right there."

7 Marta said, "Thanks, Dad! This is a much better idea than a bath. We'll have a good time and get the dogs clean, too."

Reading and Thinking

1. What did Marta think was

   better than a bath? _____

   _____

2. Why did Marta's dad help her

   call Mike? _____

   _____

Put each word in the right blank.

   belongs   mud   swimsuit

3. Flash has _____ on him.

4. This book _____ to Allen.

5. My _____ is too big.

Working with Words

Fill in the missing vowel (a, i, or o) so each sentence makes sense.

1. You did a f____ne job.

2. Wash off with the h____se.

3. We will m____ke the bed.

Use the underlined words to make a new word to finish each sentence.

4. A suit that you wear when you

   swim is called a _____.

5. A yard that is in back of a

   house is called a _____.

Circle the best word for each sentence. Then write it in the blank.

6. Do not _____ at me.
   show   shout   chair

7. Our house is _____.
   boat   clean   stay

Inky Gets the Milk

Do you sometimes watch television on Saturday morning?

¹ It was Saturday morning. Marta and her pets were watching television. Marta sat in a big chair eating her breakfast as she watched. Her big dish of Honey Corns was gone. Now she was eating an apple.

² Inky found his ball and pushed it with his paw. Nicky barked and started to chase the ball. Marta picked it up, and said, "No, Nicky. Don't bark. Mom and Dad are still sleeping, so we have to be quiet. You sit here with me and watch television."

³ On television a cat with a hat was trying every way it could to get milk. It did lots of tricks. Not one of them worked. The funny cat was so hungry, but it couldn't get any milk.

⁴ Then Marta heard a lapping sound. She looked down to see Inky with his paws on the Honey Corns dish, drinking as fast as he could.

⁵ Marta said, "Inky, you should be on television. You could show that hungry cat a new trick so it could get some milk!"

Reading and Thinking

Put each word in the right blank.

quiet lapping television

1. The cat is _____ up the milk.

2. What _____ show do you like best?

3. We were _____ in the library.

4. This story is mostly about
   ____ Inky's trick.
   ____ Mom and Dad needing quiet.
   ____ Nicky wants to play.

Working with Words

To make a word mean more than one, add -es if the word ends in s, ss, ch, sh, or x. Write these words so that they mean more than one.

1. lunch _____

2. dish _____

3. box _____

Fill in the missing letter so the sentence makes sense.

4. I like to h____lp my dad.

5. Nicky j____mped into the water.

6. Marta p____cked up the ball.

Fill in the missing letters so each sentence makes sense.

ar   or   ur

7. Did Nicky h_____t her paw?

8. Can we play in your y_____d?

Keep Away

How does Marta help her mom and dad?

1 Nicky and Marta were in the basement playing keep-away with an old football. Marta chased Nicky, but Nicky never let her take the ball. Each time Marta got near, Nicky ran faster. It was great fun!

2 Dad was not pleased with them. He and Mom were trying to paint an old table. "Marta, when you and Nicky run, you make the dust fly up. If your mother and I paint in dusty air, the paint will not look good. Please play outside until dinner."

3 Marta said, "All right, Dad."

4 Marta's mom and dad worked until the painting was done. Then Mom said, "It looks good to me."

5 Dad said, "Me, too," so they started to clean the brushes. As they came upstairs, Marta's dad said to her mom, "I must use the telephone. Why don't you take your bath first?"

6 Mom looked out at Marta and Nicky playing in the backyard. She laughed. "They can play keep-away with the football, but they can't keep away from the mud. I think they need the first baths."

Knowing the Words

Write the story words that have these meanings.

1. part of
a house _____
(Par. 1)

2. close _____
(Par. 1)

3. to wash off _____
(Par. 5)

4. top part
of a house _____
(Par. 5)

5. place in
back of a house _____
(Par. 6)

Circle the three words in each line that belong together.

6. upstairs   idea   house   kitchen

7. chair   table   mail   picture

8. box   brush   broom   mop

9. ran   sat   raced   chased

Reading and Thinking

1. If you paint in dusty air, how

will the paint look? _____

_____

2. How did Marta's mom and dad's work look when it was done?

_____

Look at each picture and circle the sentence that goes with it.

3. Dad paints
with a brush.

Dad is
brushing Nicky.

4. Joe helps
at home.

Joe is not
helping.

Marta Helps at Home

Read to find out how Marta helps.

1 "This is great soup," said Marta one night at dinner. "I would like some more, please. Who made it?"

2 Mom gave Dad a warm smile and said, "Well, I put it together while your father fixed breakfast. Then he cooked it all day. Who would you say made it?"

3 Marta said, "I think the two of you did." She ate some more soup. Then after a while she said, "I know what. If I do the dishes, then everyone in the family will have helped with dinner!"

4 Marta's dad said, "That would be great. Thanks, Marta."

5 After dinner Mom and Dad went to sit in the backyard. Marta started cleaning up the kitchen and washing the dishes. Later when her dad came inside, she was still hard at work. "What, still not done?" he asked.

6 Marta said, "Almost, Dad. Here are the last things." She picked the pets' dishes out of the water and set them in the window to dry. As she let the water out, Marta said, "Now every dish in the house is clean!"

Reading and Thinking

1. Where did Mom and Dad go after dinner? _____

2. Marta wanted to do the dishes because _____

   _____.

3. Write **1, 2,** and **3** to show what happened first, next, and last.

   ____ Marta washed the dinner dishes.

   ____ Marta washed the pets' dishes.

   ____ Marta had dinner.

Working with Words

In each rcw, circle the two letters in each word that make the same sound you hear in the underlined word.

toy p(oi)nt b(oy) n(oi)se

1. show know own throw
2. see tree feet please
3. found down around brown
4. mean need near read

Circle the best word for each sentence. Then write it in the blank.

5. Do you like this _____?

   same game name

6. Mike found _____ money.

   hit him his

7. This is my _____ hat.

   best nest last

8. Marta hit the _____.

   ball call tell

Circle each c that stands for the sound of s in these words.

9. once   12. piece
10. doctor   13. because
11. fence   14. come

Bigfoot's Lesson

Read to see if Mr. Barker knows much about dogs.

1   Mr. Barker was walking home from the pet store. He saw Marta and Lee working with Bigfoot in the park. He stood and watched.

2   "Bigfoot," Marta was saying, "this is the last hot dog. Could you please do it right?"

3   Lee said, "Bigfoot, heel." Bigfoot walked around Lee and sat by her left foot. But then he started to lean on Lee. Lee said, "No!" and pushed. But Bigfoot still leaned.

4   When the children sat down, Mr. Barker walked up and said, "Hello. May I train Bigfoot for a while?"

5   "Yes, please do," said Lee.

6   Mr. Barker stood in front of the dog and said, "Bigfoot, heel!" Bigfoot walked around to Mr. Barker's left foot. Again he started to lean.

7   Mr. Barker moved to one side. Then he pulled down on the dog's collar. Bigfoot fell over on his side and snorted. He was not hurt, but he did not like that!

8   Mr. Barker said, "Do that when he leans on you, and he will soon stop."

Knowing the Words

Write the story words that have these meanings.

1. push on

   _____
   (Par. 3)

2. what a dog has
   around its neck _____
   (Par. 7)

3. made a noise
   in the nose _____
   (Par. 7)

Circle the three words in each line that belong together.

4. mail   library   store   park
5. heel   sit   stay   found
6. collar   leash   tag   bird
7. move   walk   run   stay

Reading and Thinking

Look at each picture and circle the sentence that goes with it.

1. Dogs and cats
   do not like
   each other.

   The dog and
   cat are
   friends.

2. Marta likes to
   read books.

   Marta never
   reads books.

3. Why did Bigfoot snort?

   _____

   _____

4. Why do you think Mr. Barker
   knows a lot about dogs?

   _____

   _____

65

Plans for the Show

What should you do to set up a dog show?

1 Marta's friends met at her house one day to make plans for the dog show.

2 Mike said, "The first thing we need to do is make our signs. Can we do that today?"

3 Marta's mother came into the room to work on the signs with the children. First she helped them write on a clean piece of paper. Then she colored some dogs at the top. "Now," she said, "you need to make your copies. Then you can put them up at school and in some stores."

4 Lee said, "Dad can take me to the library tonight. I will buy the copies, and we can put them up tomorrow."

5 Marta said, "We'll need other things for the show, too. We need enough rope to make a fence around the ring."

6 "And number signs for everyone in the show," Allen said.

7 "We'll need ribbons and prizes, too!" said Christy.

8 "It will take a lot of work. But I can tell it's going to be a great show," said Marta.

Reading and Thinking

1. This story is mostly about

_____ the prize ribbons.

_____ going to the library.

_____ the dog show.

2. What five things do the children need for their dog show?

_____

_____

_____

_____

_____

3. Who will make the copies?

_____

Working with Words

Circle the right letters for each sentence. Then write them in the blank.

1. Do you w_____k hard?

ar   or   ir

2. It is your t_____n to play.

ar   or   ur

3. The dog sn_____ts loudly.

er   or   ar

Circle the best word for each sentence. Then write it in the blank.

4. Can you make your _____?

bag   bed   big

5. Mike wrote a _____.

listen   last   letter

6. We filled the _____ with milk.

pan   pet   pop

Use the underlined words to make a new word to finish each sentence.

7. <u>Corn</u> that can <u>pop</u> when you

cook it is _____.

8. A <u>walk</u> that is by the <u>side</u> of

the street is a _____.

Dad's Plans

What sometimes happens when you talk to someone who is working?

1   That night while Marta was brushing Nicky, she asked, "Dad, what should we give for prizes? Do you have any good ideas?"

2   Mom started to quiet Marta, but Dad had looked up from his work at the kitchen table. "I couldn't hear you. What did you say?"

3   Marta said, "What do you think we should give for prizes?"

4   "Oh, for your dog show. Well, blue ribbons would be nice. Look, Marta, I really need to have this work done by the time my airplane goes in the morning. We'll talk before you go to bed, all right? I should be done then."

5   "Sure, Dad, I'll be quiet," Marta said as she took Nicky outside. She sat on the steps and brushed Nicky for a short time. Then a terrible thought came to her. She called into the kitchen, "Dad, do you have to go away the day of the show?"

6   "Marta, I asked you . . . ," Dad answered. Then he said, "No, Marta. I will be right here that day. I would not miss your dog show."

Reading and Thinking

1. Why did Marta ask if Dad had to go away the day of the show?

_____

_____

_____

Fill in the blanks.

2. Mom and Dad talked as they painted.
They stands for

_____.

3. Marta's dad answered, and he said, "No, Marta."

_He_ stands for _____.

Working with Words

The missing word in each sentence sounds like _new_. Change the _n_ in _new_ to _bl, fl,_ and _thr._ Write the new words, and put them in the right sentences.

1. _____ _____ _____

2. The wind _____ hard.

3. I _____ my dog a ball.

4. The bird _____ away.

Circle the best word for each sentence. Then write it in the blank.

5. Marta will _____ Nicky.

   grass   brush   growl

6. Will Dad _____ to be here?

   dry   play   try

The ending **-er** means "more" and the ending **-est** means "most." Add the endings **-er** and **-est** to these base words.

	-er	-est
clean	_cleaner_	_cleanest_
7. kind	_____	_____
8. fast	_____	_____

Helping Friends

How can Marta and Mrs. Peters help each other?

1 Marta was watering the grass. She saw Mike's grandmother out in the yard working in her flowers. Mrs. Peters would cut a flower. Then she would bend down to put it into a basket at her feet.

2 She looked tired when she put her hands to her back and stood up. Mrs. Peters saw Marta and waved. Then she called, "Hello, Marta, how are you today?"

3 "I'm fine, Mrs. Peters. May I hold that basket for you?"

4 "Why, yes, Marta. How kind of you."

5 As they worked, Marta said, "Your flowers are beautiful this year."

6 "Thank you, Marta. I've worked hard at keeping the weeds out." Mrs. Peters then asked, "Is everything ready for your dog show?"

7 Marta was glad she had asked. "Well, almost everything. Do you know where we can get some blue ribbons that don't cost much?"

8 Mrs. Peters said, "Why, yes, I think I could make them if everyone helped me. That won't cost much!" Marta and Mrs. Peters looked at each other and smiled.

Knowing the Words

Write the story words that have these meanings.

1. to lean over

_____
(Par. 1)

2. moved hand up and down

_____
(Par. 2)

3. thinking of others

_____
(Par. 4)

Put a check by the meaning that fits the underlined word in each sentence.

4. <u>Why</u> did Mom say that?

_____ a word that asks something

_____ a word of surprise

5. <u>Why</u>, Marta, that's beautiful!

_____ a word that asks something

_____ a word of surprise

Reading and Thinking

Put each word in the right blank.

waved   bend   tired

1. Those jobs make me _____.

2. I _____ to my friend.

3. The flowers will _____ in the wind._____

4. How are Marta and Mrs. Peters helping each other?

_____

_____

_____

_____

The Signs Are Ready

What did Lee do to get the signs ready?

1 The next day everyone met at Lee's house to see the signs. Mike said, "They look great, Lee. How much did they cost?"

2 Lee said, "They didn't cost us a thing. I helped my aunt wash her car, so she made the copies for us."

3 Marta said, "Great, Lee!" and shook her hand.

4 Allen was delighted and said, "That's good, but how did they get so shiny?"

5 Lee looked even prouder. "My aunt has a spray that she uses on her pictures. We sprayed all the signs with it, so they can't get wet and muddy if it rains."

6 Christy said, "That was a wonderful idea, Lee."

7 Joe said, "You really used your head."

8 Mike nodded. Then he said, "Do we need to buy your aunt another can of that spray now?"

9 Lee smiled and answered, "No, it didn't take much. And Aunt Ming wants to help us all she can because she is going to enter her dog, Toy, in our dog show!"

Reading and Thinking

Look at each picture and circle the sentence that goes with it.

1. Nicky is asleep in her basket.

   Nicky has a bone.

2. Inky is jumping.

   Inky is drinking milk.

3. Mike cuts the grass.

   Mike weeds the flowers.

Put each word in the right blank.

spray   shiny   enter

4. Marta has _____ new shoes.

5. We _____ the flowers.

6. Please knock and _____.

Working with Words

Write these words so that they mean more than one.

1. sign   _____

2. idea   _____

3. can   _____

Circle the best word for each sentence. Then write it in the blank.

4. Dad _____ breakfast.
   cooking   cooked

5. Mom is _____ outside.
   works   working

6. Grandfather _____ to help.
   wants   wanting

7. We can plant a _____.
   good   garden   judge

8 Do you live in the _____?
   coat   city   cut

9. Please _____ me go.
   let   lot   last

10. She has a funny _____.
   hat   hit   hot

Good Places for Signs

Where is a good place to put up a dog show sign?

1   Marta moved closer to the sleeping dog. "Nicky, do you want to take a walk?" she asked softly. Nicky's eyes opened at once. The dog barked, jumped up, and wiggled with delight.

2   Marta laughed, "I think you do! Come on. We'll go put up our signs for the show."

3   Everyone Marta asked was glad to have a sign. Soon she had only one sign left. Where could she put it? Then she saw the pet store and thought, "That would be a good place."

4   Marta and Nicky walked inside and found Mike talking to Mr. Barker. When Mike saw Marta, he asked, "Do you have any signs left? I don't have any more, and Mr. Barker needs one. Guess what? Mr. Barker is going to give us some dog toys to use for prizes! They won't cost us a thing. All we have to do is say that they came from his pet store when we give them out."

5   Marta laughed, "That's great, Mike. Mr. Barker has been a big help. Could he be the judge for our show, too?"

Reading and Thinking

1. Why would the pet shop be a good place for a dog show sign?

   _____

   _____

   _____

2. To tell where the prizes came from at the show, Mike will say, "Today's prizes are from

   _____

   _____ ".

3. Do you think Mr. Barker will be

   a good judge for the show? ___

   Why do you think so? _____

   _____

   _____

Working with Words

Circle the best word for each sentence. Then write it in the blank.

1. What is _____ than a bath?
   basket   basement   better

2. Please _____ your work.
   check   collar   closet

Write these sentences. Use one shorter word for the two words that are underlined.

3. I do not have a sign.

   _____

4. That is great!

   _____

5. We will be glad.

   _____

6. That is not a good place.

   _____

Beautiful Ribbons

What will the children buy to make prize ribbons?

1 At ten the next morning, Mike and Marta sat in the park with one of their signs. Ten people signed up for the show. Not everyone entered each class, but most entered more than one. Mike and Marta had a can of money when they left the park.

2 They walked right over to Mike's house. "Mrs. Peters," Marta said, "we have money to buy things now. Will you help us buy the things we need to make the ribbons?"

3 Mrs. Peters said, "I surely will. I've been thinking, and I know just what we need."

4 Soon Mike, Marta, and Mrs. Peters were inside the store. Marta had never been there before. She was surprised to see so many things. The salesperson showed them ribbons in many colors. Mike said, "Why don't we get blue for first, red for second, and white for third. We have enough money. If we want to give more prizes, we could buy more colors."

5 Mrs. Peters said, "Good idea. We'll get this box of gold glitter too. This will make beautiful prize ribbons."

Reading and Thinking

Put each word in the right blank.

entered   glitter   prizes

1. This _____ will make the ribbon shiny.

2. Lee _____ her dog in the show.

3. We will give ribbons for

   _____.

4. How did Mike and Marta get a can full of money? _____

   _____

   _____

Working with Words

Sometimes the letter c stands for the sound s makes as in *city*. Circle each c that stands for the sound of s in these words.

1. circle   3. city
2. cat   4. car

Circle the best word for each sentence. Then write it in the blank.

5. I know _____ you want.

   what   shut   that

6. I'll be _____ in a minute.

   chair   there   where

7. The _____ blew hard.

   will   well   wind

8. Please _____ my dish.

   fall   fell   fill

Mom Helps the Show

How does Marta's mom help?

1   The next day at the park, Mike and Joe got four more people signed up. The boys took the money they got to Marta's house. Marta's mother said, "Good work. I'll put this away for now. Do you know if Marta got permission from the city to use the park for this show?"

2   With big eyes, Mike said, "No."

3   Joe said, "We didn't even think of that."

4   Marta's mom nodded and said, "Well, I will look into it. Don't say a thing about it for a while.

5   But Mike and Joe couldn't help looking at each other while they helped Marta and Mrs. Peters with the ribbons. Marta and Mrs. Peters were hard at work and didn't even see the looks.

6   Mrs. Peters made a big "5" in paste on a green ribbon. She handed it to Marta, who shook gold glitter on the paste. Marta said, "These will be the best ribbons a dog show ever had!"

7   Just then Mom came in to say, "I called and asked for permission to have the dog show at the park. They say we can use the park at no cost!"

Reading and Thinking

Put each word in the right blank.

permission   paste   nodded

1. Marta _____ her head.

2. I have _____ to go.

3. _____ will make the ribbon stick together.

4. Who called the people who run the park? _____

5. How do you think Mike and Joe felt while they were helping with the ribbons? _____

_____

Learning to Study

Write each set of words in A-B-C order.

1. people   money   other

_____

_____

_____

2. busy   paste   cost

_____

_____

_____

3. glitter   ribbon   city

_____

_____

_____

Nicky Remembers a Friend

Read to see whom Nicky remembers.

1 Marta and Mike were in the basement working on big number signs. They were hard at work because everyone who entered a dog in the show would need a sign. Mom knocked on the door and said, "Marta, look who is here!" A bright-eyed woman walked into the room.

2 "Grandmother!" shouted Marta. She ran to give her a hug.

3 "This must be Nicky," said Marta's grandmother as she leaned over to pet Nicky's head. "You are right, Marta. She looks like a wonderful dog." Nicky was sniffing Grandmother's coat.

4 Then Marta's grandfather entered the room and said, "See who came with us, Marta." Nicky started to bark and jump up. She was trying to get past Grandmother.

5 Marta's mom said, "Nicky, what is wrong with you? Now stop that!"

6 Then a woman said, "Nicky, sit!"

7 At once Nicky sat down, and Marta said, "It's Aunt Rosa!"

8 Aunt Rosa said, "Are you surprised to see me? You should know I would not miss seeing you and Nicky in the dog show tomorrow."

Reading and Thinking

1. Who made the number signs?

   _____

2. What do you think Nicky was sniffing on Grandmother's coat?

   _____

3. Write **1, 2,** and **3** to show what happened first, next, and last.

   ____ Aunt Rosa said, "Nicky, sit!"

   ____ Grandfather talked to Marta.

   ____ Mom knocked on Marta's door.

Working with Words

In each sentence, circle the word that is made of two shorter words. Write the two words on the lines.

(Everyone) met at Lee's house.

Every   *one*

1. Do you ever play football?

   _____   _____

2. Grandmother gave Marta a hug.

   _____   _____

Circle the best word for each sentence. Then write it in the blank.

3. They played with _____ toys.

   chair   their   where

4. I am _____ in line.

   while   short   third

In each row, circle the two letters in each word that stand for the vowel sound you hear in the underlined word.

5. <u>day</u>   paint   train   stay
6. <u>each</u>   green   mean   feet
7. <u>know</u>   coat   show   own
8. <u>proud</u>   down   about   now

81

The Dog Show

Will Marta get nervous when she does something in front of a crowd?

¹ After drying her hands, Marta took up Nicky's leash again. The waiting was hard for Marta. She was nervous, but Nicky was not. Nicky looked up at her and wiggled with delight. Nicky liked this crowd of people and dogs. Marta petted her and gave her a little smile. It was almost their turn.

² She saw Lee and Bigfoot standing with Aunt Ming and Toy. Christy and Joe were there, waiting their turns in the ring. Allen was holding his puppy, Paws. He waved to Marta. "Great dog show," he called, and Marta waved back.

³ Marta's grandmother came up to her and gave her a little hug. "Try to look like this is lots of fun, Marta," she said quietly. "Don't let Nicky get nervous."

⁴ Everyone clapped for Mike and Flash as they walked out of the ring. Marta smiled at Mike. Then Mr. Barker, the judge, said, "Number ten, you may start."

⁵ Marta said, "Nicky, heel." All eyes were on them as they walked into the ring.

Knowing the Words

Write the story words that have these meanings.

1. afraid

_____
(Par. 1)

2. a number of people together

_____
(Par. 1)

3. place for a dog show

_____
(Par. 5)

Put a check by the meaning that fits the underlined word in each sentence.

4. Marta <u>saw</u> Lee standing there.

____ something that cuts wood

____ used her eyes

5. Marta walked into the <u>ring</u>.

____ sound a telephone makes

____ a circle where a show is

Reading and Thinking

Put each word in the right blank.

crowd   judge   nervous

1. The _____ of people clapped.

2. Who will _____ the dog show?

3. She is _____ about the show.

4. How did Nicky feel at the dog show? _____

_____

5. How do you think Nicky and Marta will do in the show?

_____

Gold Ribbon Winner

Who will win the gold ribbon?

1 Mr. Barker quieted everyone. He said, "We have one more prize to give. All of you now in the ring have won ribbons today. Now one of you will win a gold ribbon."

2 Gold ribbon? Marta looked in surprise at Mrs. Peters, who was holding up a gold ribbon.

3 The judge said, "All of the dogs here are well trained. I can't pick a winner. I will now ask each dog to show us a trick. When the crowd claps the most, that dog wins the gold ribbon."

4 Allen had Paws jump on two feet. Mike had Flash turn over and over. Lee rode on top of Bigfoot. Joe had his dog, Ears, stand on his back feet, and Christy had Shoes bark different ways. Other dogs did other tricks. Then, last of all, it was Marta's turn.

5 Marta was glad she had worked on a special trick with Nicky. She said, "Nicky, stay." Then Marta walked into the ring. She lay down on her back and called, "Nicky, racehorse!" All eyes were on Nicky as she ran to Marta as fast as she could. Then Nicky jumped over Marta from her head to her feet! The crowd clapped hard, and Nicky was the gold ribbon winner!

Reading and Thinking

1. Why couldn't Mr. Barker pick a

   winner? _____

   _____

   _____

2. What makes you think that
   Marta did not know about the
   gold ribbon?

   _____

   _____

3. Why did the crowd pick Nicky

   to win? _____

   _____

Working with Words

Circle the best word for each
sentence. Then write it in the
blank.

1. I am still _____ for
   Nicky.

   clapped   clapping

2. Nicky _____ over Marta.

   jumped   jumping

Add 's to these words to show
what belongs to each one. Write
the new word.

3. judge   _____ smile

4. Marta   _____ turn

5. Nicky   _____ ribbon

Circle g when it stands for the
sound of g in go.

6. good   8. judge
7. garden   9. again

The Forest Story Teller

How did Uncle Bunny learn to write?

1 Bless my ears and whiskers! I'm so glad I learned to write! When I was just a young rabbit, a school was near my house. One day I saw a box under a window at the school. I climbed on top and listened. The children were learning to write.

2 "They can learn with such little ears," I said to myself. "Maybe I can learn as well with my big ears!"

3 So each day I climbed up to the window to watch and listen. At night I practiced writing in the snow.

4 "What funny tracks!" said Red Squirrel one evening.

5 "These tracks are writing," I said. "Writing uses things called letters. These letters say Red Squirrel."

6 I began with letters and short words. Soon I thought about writing some short stories.

7 Other friends came to watch. They began calling me Uncle Funny Bunny. I'm still funny, but now they just call me Uncle Bunny. They are happy that I wrote the stories in this book about them. I hope you'll be just as glad.

Knowing the Words

Write the words from the story that have these meanings.

1. face hairs _____
(Par. 1)

2. did over and over _____
(Par. 3)

3. did write _____
(Par. 7)

Working with Words

Circle the right word to finish the sentence. Then write the word in the blank.

1. The team ran a good _____.

(face, case, race)

2. Hit the ball with the _____.

(bell, bat, bed)

Reading and Thinking

1. Check the answer that tells what the story is mostly about.

_____ how children learn

_____ Uncle Bunny's big ears

_____ how Uncle Bunny learned to write

2. Look at the picture. Check the two sentences that tell about the picture.

_____ Uncle Bunny wears glasses.

_____ Uncle Bunny drives a car.

_____ Uncle Bunny can write.

3. Uncle Bunny found a box under a

_____.

Some things are real and some are make-believe. Write **R** by real things. Write **M** by make-believe things.

4. _____ Rabbits can write.

5. _____ Children can learn.

6. _____ Squirrels can talk.

Thunder and Rain

If you were a deer caught in a storm, where would you go?

1   I was eating lunch in the clover field when the sky turned very dark. Thunder rumbled all around. "Rabbits crabbits!" I thought as I ran for home. "It was going to be such a good lunch."

2   On my way through the field I saw Mrs. Whitetail and Spotty, my deer friends. I wondered why they were not hurrying home. "Mrs. Whitetail," I called, "didn't you hear the thunder?"

3   "Yes, we were under the trees when we heard it," she called back. "Spotty tried to run away. But we must stay quiet in a storm. Rain in the trees makes so much noise. We must be still and listen for danger.

4   "We'll rest here in the open field until the storm passes. Then we'll return to the trees. We may get wet, but we'll be safe."

5   "Bless my ears and whiskers!" I cried. "I don't like to get wet. I'm going home to keep dry and think about the lunch I'm missing." Oh, well, maybe the clover will be even better after the rain.

Knowing the Words

Write the words from the story that have these meanings.

1. kind of plant _____
   (Par. 1)

2. storm sound _____
   (Par. 1)

3. loud sounds _____
   (Par. 3)

The words *come* and *go* have meanings so different that they are **opposite.** Make a line from each word in the first list to the word in the second list with the opposite meaning.

4. wet   noise

5. quiet   dry

6. stay   leave

Working with Words

A word without any endings is a **base word.** The base word of *talking* is *talk.* Circle each base word below.

1. listens 2. pushed 3. eating

Sometimes one word stands for two words. The word *didn't* stands for *did not.* Write a word from the story that can stand for each pair of words.

4. we will _____
   (Par. 4)

5. I am _____
   (Par. 5)

Reading and Thinking

1. Check the answer that tells what the story is mostly about.

   _____ Uncle Bunny having lunch

   _____ where animals go during a storm

   _____ black clouds

2. Where were Mrs. Whitetail and Spotty when they heard thunder?

   _____

3. Check the sentence that tells why the deer moved to the open field.

   _____ They went there to eat.

   _____ Spotty tried to run away.

   _____ A storm was coming.

4. Why do you think Spotty tried to run away? _____

   _____

89

The Haircut

Why do you think Sniffles felt so bad about his haircut?

1   I was on my way to the carrot patch one morning when I heard a sad little voice. It sounded like my friend Sniffles.

2   The sound was like crying. I decided to see if I could help. I followed the voice and came to the pond. There was Sniffles. That little lamb was sitting by the pond. He was looking at himself in the water.

3   "What is wrong, Sniffles?" I asked. "Why are you crying?"

4   "Just look at me, Uncle Bunny!" he said. Then he cried even louder.

"I didn't know being a lamb would mean losing my wool every spring."

5   "Think about how your wool will help keep people warm," I said. "It will make coats and hats and gloves. Doesn't that make you happy?"

6   "Yes," he answered, "but I need to keep warm, too. And I look so funny without my coat."

7   "Your coat will start to grow back very soon," I said. "In the summer you will like being cool."

8   "I guess you are right, Uncle Bunny," Sniffles said. "Maybe it's just that this was my very first haircut."

Knowing the Words

Write the words from the story that have these meanings.

1. a small place _____
   (Par. 1)

2. hair cut from sheep _____
   (Par. 4)

3. between cold and warm _____
   (Par. 7)

Circle the three words in each row that belong together.

4. morning   year   night   afternoon

5. coats   hats   feet   shoes

6. wet   cold   warm   hot

7. happy   sad   angry   old

Learning to Study

Number the words to show A-B-C order for each list.

1. ____ lamb
   ____ carrot
   ____ friend
   ____ wool

2. ____ cool
   ____ answered
   ____ patch
   ____ wrote

Reading and Thinking

1. Check the answer that tells what the story is mostly about.

   ____ keeping people warm

   ____ being cool in the summer

   ____ Sniffles giving his wool

2. What was Sniffles doing by the pond? _____

   _____

3. Sniffles thought he looked funny because _____

   _____.

Words such as *he, his, she,* and *her* take the place of other words. Read these sentences. Fill in the blanks.

4. Sniffles cried as he saw himself.

   He stands for _____.

5. Uncle Bunny ate his carrots.

   His stands for _____.

Write **R** by the real things. Write **M** by the make-believe things.

6. ____ Lambs wear gloves.

7. ____ Coats are made from wool.

The Tree Planter

Why do squirrels put away food?

1 One winter morning I heard lots of angry chattering. I hopped over the hill toward the noise. Red Squirrel was almost standing on his head in the snow. He was digging as fast as he was chattering. "Just let me catch that thief! I'll show that one a thing or two!"

2 Red stopped digging and looked up. He waved his tail and looked angry enough to eat a rock.

3 "Someone took my acorn! I put it under this tree last fall. Now it's gone! Sorry, Uncle Bunny, but I can't talk now. I've got work to do!"

4 Red kept digging faster and faster into the snow. At last he came up with an acorn between his front teeth. "At last," he cried, "I've found my breakfast!" Then he ran up an oak tree faster than I could say, "Bless my ears and whiskers!"

5 I laughed to myself. Red Squirrel never remembers where he hides his acorns. When spring comes, they start to grow into tiny oak trees. He plants new trees without knowing it.

Knowing the Words

Write the words from the story that have these meanings.

1. one who takes something _____
   (Par. 1)

2. nut from oak tree _____
   (Par. 3)

Check the meaning that fits the underlined word in each sentence.

3. We clean up leaves in the <u>fall</u>.

   _____ part of year before winter

   _____ to drop suddenly

4. I <u>wave</u> as I leave for school.

   _____ make a good-bye sign

   _____ rolling water

Working with Words

Write **S** beside each word that stands for one of something. Write **P** by each word that stands for more than one.

1. _____ noise   2. _____ acorns

Circle the right word to finish each sentence. Then write the word in the blank.

3. The cold wind _____
   in our faces. (threw, flew, blew)

4. The cars hit with a loud _____.
   (splash, crash, flash)

Reading and Thinking

1. Red Squirrel planted an acorn in

   what part of the year? _____

Write **T** if the sentence is true.
Write **F** if it is not true.

2. _____ Oak trees grow from acorns.

3. _____ The story happens in winter.

4. Red could not find his acorn

   because _____

   _____.

5. What do you think Red did after

   he ran up the tree? _____

   _____

6. How did Red Squirrel feel when he thought someone took his nut?

   _____

The Skunks' Present

Why wouldn't anyone want a present from a skunk?

1   On my way to the carrot patch one morning, I met Mrs. Skunk and her family. She was waving her bushy tail like a flag. Behind her were six little skunks, waving their tails, too.

2   "Hello, Mrs. Skunk," I called to her. "Would you like to have breakfast with me?"

3   "Thank you, Uncle Bunny," she said. "We are on our way to look for insects."

4   Just then I heard an angry growl behind me. I turned. A big dog was running right at us.

5   "Quick, come under this berry bush with me!" I called. "The branches will keep us safe." I rolled under the bush and waited for the skunk family. But the mother and her babies stayed where they were. Mrs. Skunk started dancing her front feet up and down. The little skunks danced, too. Suddenly Mrs. Skunk and her little ones turned their backs and waved their tails.

6   That big dog stopped so fast. Then he turned and hurried away.

7   "Rabbits crabbits," I thought to myself. "I should have guessed what would happen. Even that dog wanted to stay away from the skunk smell!"

Knowing the Words

Write the words from the story that have these meanings.

1. black and
white animal _____
(Par. 1)

2. small animals such
as bees and ants _____
(Par. 3)

Words that mean the same or nearly the same are called **synonyms.** Circle two synonyms in each row.

3. begin   stop   call   start

4. bird   rabbit   skunk   bunny

5. listen   catch   see   look

6. run   car   hurry   dog

Learning to Study

Number the words to show A-B-C order for each list.

1. ____ turn

____ patch

____ bee

____ skunk

2. ____ carrot

____ growl

____ happen

____ safe

Reading and Thinking

1. Check the answer that tells what the story is mostly about.

____ how rabbits hide under berry bushes

____ a frightened dog

____ how skunks keep safe

2. Number the sentences to show what happened first, second, third, and last.

____ The skunks danced.

____ Uncle Bunny heard a growl.

____ The dog ran away.

____ Uncle Bunny met the skunks.

Write the best word to finish each sentence below.

3. We heard the band and wanted

to _____. (read, dance, believe)

4. The dog _____ at the loud noise. (growled, worked, laughed)

Make Way for Betsy

Why does Betsy like to climb trees?

1   Betsy Bear's path runs from a tall tree down to the stream. One day I found out why she has the path.

2   Betsy was climbing the tree. She pulled herself up and put one paw around the tree. She stuck her other paw into a hole in the tree. Then she pulled her paw out and licked it.

3   Suddenly I heard a buzzing sound. Bees lived inside the tree. Betsy was taking some of their honey! Angry bees buzzed around Betsy, but her fur kept her safe.

4   Before long some of the bees flew toward her face. Betsy gave a loud "Woof!" A bee gave her a sting right on her nose where she had no fur. Betsy shook her head and cried as she hurried down the tree.

5   Betsy hit the ground hard. All she could think of was her nose. She ran down the path toward the stream as bees flew after her. Splash! She jumped into the stream. The water came up around her burning nose.

6   Now I'm always careful to stay off Betsy's path. I would not want to be in the way when she needs it!

Knowing the Words

Write the words from the story that have these meanings.

1. a place to walk _____
    (Par. 1)

2. insect bite _____
    (Par. 4)

In each row, circle the two words with opposite meanings.

3. inside   little   claws   outside

4. long   push   hungry   pull

Working with Words

An 's at the end of a word may be used to show that something belongs to someone. Add 's to each name. Write each name in the right blank.

Uncle Bunny_____   Betsy Bear_____

1. _____ burning nose

2. _____ whiskers

Circle the right word to finish each sentence. Then write the word in the blank.

3. Please _____ your book
    with you. (bring, string, spring)

4. The clothes are _____.
    (clean, cream, string)

Reading and Thinking

1. Where did Betsy's path go?

    _____

2. What did Betsy find inside the

    tree? _____

3. The bees were angry because

    _____.

Write **T** if the sentence is true.
Write **F** if it is not true.

4. _____ Bears and bees eat honey.

5. _____ Bears and bees make
          honey.

6. _____ Bees are larger than bears.

7. What do you think Betsy did when
    she came out of the stream?

    _____

    _____

97

A Narrow Escape

How can a rabbit trick a fox?

1   I try to keep away from Tricky and Slick Fox. Sometimes that isn't easy. Once I was hopping toward the meadow when I heard a pit-pat behind me. I hopped a little faster. The pit-pats came a little faster. When I stopped the pit-pats stopped. I looked back. There was Tricky in the middle of the path!

2   Rabbits crabbits! There wasn't much space between Tricky and me. I tossed my cane away and raced as fast as I could. I flew so fast my feet hardly touched the ground. The wind whistled past my ears. My whiskers blew against my face.

3   Then I saw something under a bush ahead. It was Slick. Tricky was chasing me to Slick's hiding place.

4   Just as Slick moved out from under the bush, I knew what to do. I closed my eyes and jumped with all my might. I sailed over Slick's head. I landed in a patch of bushes far away from the two foxes.

5   Tricky was running so fast he couldn't stop. He and Slick ran right into each other. I hopped away toward home. I guess that's one time the foxes tricked each other.

Knowing the Words

Write the words from the story that have these meanings.

1. grassy field _____

(Par. 1)

2. very close to _____

(Par. 2)

Check the meaning that fits the underlined word in each sentence.

3. The kite <u>sailed</u> above the trees.

_____ moved on water

_____ flew high

4. Joe is putting a <u>patch</u> on his coat.

_____ place where carrots grow

_____ small piece of cloth

Working with Words

Write a word from the story that stands for each pair of words.

1. was not _____

(Par. 2)

2. could not _____

(Par. 5)

Reading and Thinking

1. Check two sentences that tell how Uncle Bunny and the foxes were the same.

_____ They were all clever.

_____ They were all afraid.

_____ They were all good runners.

2. What did Uncle Bunny throw away before he ran? _____

3. Where was Tricky chasing Uncle Bunny? _____

_____

4. When Uncle Bunny saw Tricky behind him, he may have felt

_____.

Write the best word to finish each sentence below.

5. The fox _____ over the fence. (sang, jumped, sat)

6. The wind blew the _____ off the trees. (mountain, leaves, sun)

7. The runner was so _____ she seemed to fly. (slow, new, fast)

The String House

What did Uncle Bunny think about the string house?

1 Sometimes I like to take a walk in the woods. The sun is so warm when it shines down through the trees.

2 On one afternoon walk, I saw something that looked like glass strings. When I got closer the strings seemed tied together. I looked again and saw something move. One of the strings dropped straight down from a high branch. Something bounced at the end of the string.

3 The bouncing thing turned out to be Willy Webb, a friendly spider.

4 "I'm working on my new house, Uncle Bunny," Willy said, as I came closer. "How do you like it?"

5 "I never saw a house like that," I answered. "How can you tell the rooms apart, and how can anyone walk around in it?"

6 "It's just one big room," he said. "My long legs are just right for this kind of house. And I should call it by its real name. We spiders have a different name for our houses. We call them webs."

7 "I guess that means your house is Webb's web!" I laughed.

8 "That's funny, Uncle Bunny," Willy said. "A web is a good house for me. I can build it all by myself. If I want to move, I can build a new one. And it can also help me catch my dinner."

Knowing the Words

Write the words from the story that have these meanings.

1. sends out light _____
    (Par. 1)

2. between _____
    (Par. 1)

3. moving up and down _____
    (Par. 3)

4. small animal
    that builds webs _____
    (Par. 3)

5. homes for spiders _____
    (Par. 6)

Circle the three words in each row that belong together.

6. spider   frog   ant   bee

7. airplane   sun   moon   star

8. tell   say   carry   talk

9. small   long   high   tall

Working with Words

Walk and *talk* are **rhyming words.** In rhyming words, only the beginning sound is different. Change the *f* in *fine* to *l, m,* or *n* to make rhyming words. Write each new word.

1. _____

2. _____

3. _____

Reading and Thinking

Words such as *he, she,* and *it* take the place of other words. Read these sentences. Then fill in the blanks.

1. Willy sang as he worked. *He*

    stands for _____.

2. Willy's house moved as it caught

    the wind. *It* stands for _____

    _____.

Write the best word to finish each sentence below.

3. I _____ to be at
    school on time. (ran, thought, ate)

4. The children moved the _____
    to the backyard. (street, toys,
    stairs)

5. The _____ showed we
    were late. (flag, chicken, clock)

6. Check the sentence that tells why
    Uncle Bunny would have trouble
    in Willy Webb's house.

    _____ Rabbits can't walk on
          strings.

    _____ The roof is too low.

    _____ There is only one bedroom.

Breakfast with Barnie

Find out about Barnie's breakfast.

1 One night I was resting under a tree. I was just thinking and looking up at the stars. Suddenly two of the stars blinked. Then a voice called, "Hello down there, Uncle Bunny! I just woke up and I'm ready for breakfast. Will you join me?"

2 "Bless my ears and whiskers!" I shouted. Then I sat up to look more closely. I saw that Barnie Raccoon was sitting on a branch of the tree. The two "stars" were Barnie's eyes!

3 I followed Barnie down to the stream. We crawled out onto a flat rock. Soon Barnie reached his paw into the water. With a quick move, he pulled out a wiggling fish.

4 "This one's for you," he said as he handed me the fish. Barnie's paws are like little hands. It was easy for him to hold the wiggling fish. My paws are different. I had to put the fish under one paw. Then I had to push on the fish to hold it.

5 Next, Barnie caught a fish for himself. "Now, let's wash them," he said. We leaned over. Barnie began to swish his fish in the water. Then I felt myself moving. Splash! I fell onto my head in the stream!

6 My fish swam away and I climbed out. "Barnie, I think I'll have my breakfast in the carrot patch from now on. Carrots don't wiggle!"

Knowing the Words

Write the words from the story that have these meanings.

1. lights in the sky _____
(Par. 1)

2. closed and
opened quickly _____
(Par. 1)

Write **S** for each pair of words that have the same or nearly the same meanings (synonyms). Write **O** for each pair with opposite meanings.

3. little _____ small

4. easy _____ hard

5. wash _____ clean

Circle the three words in each row that belong together.

6. raccoon   carrot   rabbit   fish

7. water   paws   eyes   head

8. branch   tree   star   leaves

Reading and Thinking

1. Number the sentences to show what happened first, second, third, and last.

_____ Barnie caught a fish.

_____ Uncle Bunny followed Barnie.

_____ Two "stars" blinked.

_____ Uncle Bunny lost his fish.

2. How were Barnie's eyes like

stars? _____

_____

3. Check the answer that tells how Barnie and Uncle Bunny are different.

_____ They both like to eat breakfast.

_____ Barnie likes fish, but Uncle Bunny likes carrots.

Write the best word to finish each sentence below.

4. The boat was _____ on the lake. (wiggling, sailing, swimming)

5. I _____ quietly past the room. (walked, rolled, blinked)

Seeing Double

What kind of strange noises did Uncle Bunny hear?

1   One afternoon I was hopping home from the carrot patch. I stopped to look at some flowers. That's when I heard a strange noise in the bushes behind me. Then I heard the sound ahead of me.

2   "Rabbits crabbits!" I thought. "Now what should I do? I don't know what it is, but it's all around me."

3   Just then a furry ball rolled onto the path. I jumped back, and the ball started laughing. Suddenly there was another furry ball behind me. It was laughing, too.

4   "I've seen some strange things in the forest," I thought to myself. "But what could this be?"

5   The furry things kept laughing harder and harder. I decided to look closer. Soon I saw that each ball had feet and a tail. One ball rolled over. A furry face appeared. It looked like a little Betsy Bear.

6   "We're sorry, Uncle Bunny," one of the furry balls said. "We didn't mean to scare you. I'm Rugs and that's my sister Hugs. We're Betsy's children."

7   "We were playing," Hugs said, "and we saw you going home. We decided to tease you."

8   "Well, you did scare me at first," I said. "But I couldn't stay afraid when you both started laughing."

Knowing the Words

Check the meaning that fits the underlined word in each sentence.

1. <u>Roll</u> the mud into a ball.

    _____ make round

    _____ a kind of bread

2. The bears like to <u>play</u> outside.

    _____ a show to watch

    _____ do a game or have fun

Use lines to match the words with opposite meanings.

3. laughing   coming

4. going   behind

5. ahead   crying

Working with Words

Write a word from the story that can stand for each pair of words.

1. it is _____
    (Par. 2)

2. we are _____
    (Par. 6)

3. that is _____
    (Par. 6)

Make each word mean more than one by adding **-s.** Write the word.

4. forest _____

5. flower _____

Reading and Thinking

Write **R** by the real things. Write **M** by the make-believe things.

1. _____ Bears laugh at rabbits.

2. _____ Bears talk to rabbits.

3. _____ Bears scare rabbits.

Write the best word to finish each sentence below.

4. The loud horn will _____ the five boys. (learn, scare, feed)

5. I'll _____ my face and brush my hair. (light, move, wash)

6. José _____ the man play the game. (watched, told, knew)

7. We planted _____ in the garden. (words, ideas, flowers)

Ruby Throat

What makes hummingbirds different from other birds?

1   The smallest bird in the woods is Ruby Throat, the hummingbird. He's the best flyer, too. He can fly like most birds. Or he can "park" in the air without going anywhere at all.

2   One afternoon I was dreaming about carrots and clover. Suddenly I felt something! There was a loud buzzing in my left ear. Then something touched my other ear.

3   "Rabbits crabbits! Who is there?" I shouted, as I shook my ears.

4   "Oh, I'm sorry, Uncle Bunny," a tiny voice said. "I must need glasses. I thought your ear was a flower!"

5   I opened my eyes. Then I saw Ruby Throat fluttering near my nose. "Maybe you should try over there," I said. I pointed to a real flower nearby. He flew to the flower and put his long beak inside. He was reaching for insects that were stuck in the flower.

6   Ruby seemed to be standing still in the air. His wings were moving so fast I couldn't see them. In a little while he backed out and flew away.

7   All at once my ears felt so tired. I thought for a minute, and then I knew why. I was trying to wave my ears as fast as Ruby Throat waved his wings.

Knowing the Words

Words that mean the same or nearly the same are called **synonyms.** Use lines to match synonyms.

1. little   quick

2. close   tiny

3. fast   near

Working with Words

A **compound word** is made by putting two words together. Write a compound word for the underlined words below. One is done for you.

A word meaning <u>some</u> kind of

<u>thing</u> is _*something*_ .

1. A time <u>after</u> the <u>noon</u> time is

_____.

2. A <u>bird</u> whose wings make a <u>humming</u> sound is a

_____.

Fill in each blank with the right pair of letters to make a word.

        ch   sh   th   wh

3. _____iskers   **6.** _____ink

4. _____is   **7.** _____ange

5. _____eel   **8.** _____ort

Reading and Thinking

1. How is a hummingbird different

from most birds? _____

_____

Write **R** by the real things. Write **M** by the make-believe things.

2. _____ Hummingbirds wear glasses.

3. _____ Hummingbirds eat insects.

4. _____ Hummingbirds are different from most birds.

5. _____ Hummingbirds wear shoes.

6. Check the answer that tells what a hummingbird nest may look like.

_____ very small

_____ a box for shoes

_____ very large

Diver Hawk

How did Diver frighten Uncle Bunny?

1   Not long ago Diver Hawk frightened me. He didn't mean to, but I was scared just the same. I was resting in a field watching the sky. As I looked up I saw Diver. His wide wings were stretched out. He seemed to be floating.

2   Suddenly Diver lifted his wings over his back. He pointed his head down and began to drop. "He's seen something for lunch," I thought.

3   He dropped faster and closer. He was coming right at me! I was so scared I couldn't move. I shut my eyes. I waited. When nothing happened, I slowly opened one eye.

4   Diver was sitting on a fence nearby. "I saw you while I was floating in the sky. You were so still I just wanted to see if you were OK."

5   "I was afraid I might be your lunch," I said, feeling much better.

6   "Oh, I usually eat things that hurt farms," Diver said. "Some people don't like me, but I really help them."

7   "Bless my ears and whiskers!" I exclaimed. "I'll write a story telling how much you help!"

Knowing the Words

Write the words from the story that have these meanings.

1. scared _____
   (Par. 1)

2. closed _____
   (Par. 3)

3. cried out _____
   (Par. 7)

Circle the three words in each row that belong together.

4. wings   head   sky   beak

5. meadow   field   lake   land

6. fit   scared   frightened   afraid

Working with Words

A **compound word** is made by putting two words together. Use these words to make two compound words.

fast   light   flash   break

1. _____

2. _____

Reading and Thinking

1. Check the answer that tells what the story is mostly about.

   _____ how Diver scared Uncle Bunny

   _____ how hawks fly

   _____ animals eating lunch

2. Write two things Diver Hawk did

   to frighten Uncle Bunny. _____

   _____

   _____

3. Write **T** if the sentence is true. Write **F** if it is not true.

   _____ The story takes place at night.

   _____ Hawks cannot see very well.

   _____ Hawks can fly very well.

Write the best word to finish each sentence below.

4. The house was _____ after the party ended. (quiet, scared, angry)

5. My sister and her _____ took a trip. (field, friends, fence)

The Night Hunter

Read about how owls can hear.

1   With my big ears I hear very well. But not long ago I found out that size of ears isn't very important. Cynthia Owl's ears don't even show, but she hears things I can't.

2   I was in the clover field for a late supper. Suddenly I heard a long "Whoo-hoo-ee-ooo." "Who's there?" I cried.

3   "It's me, Uncle Bunny. I heard another owl. I told it to stay away."

4   I looked up and saw Cynthia Owl. She was high in a tree near the field.

"Bless my ears and whiskers!" I exclaimed. "I didn't hear anyone but you. You must have very sharp ears. They are so small I can't see them."

5   "Each of my ears is a small fold of skin. It goes from each eye down to the side of my neck," she said. "I can turn my head almost around. That way I can catch sounds from everywhere. I don't even have to move the rest of me."

6   Suddenly Cynthia flew off to the corner of the field. Soon she returned to the tree carrying a mouse.

7   Rabbits crabbits! I have good ears but not like Cynthia's. My ears don't help me find clover the way hers help find a mouse.

Knowing the Words

Write the words from the story that have these meanings.

1. how big or little
something is _____
(Par. 1)

2. one more _____
(Par. 3)

3. very good, fine _____
(Par. 4)

4. place where two
sides come together _____
(Par. 6)

In each row, circle the two words with opposite meanings.

5. down   off   around   up

6. tell   gone   say   came

7. show   large   small   bless

Working with Words

Circle the right word to finish each sentence. Then write the word in the blank.

1. My mother opened a _____
of soup for lunch. (can   cane)

2. Will you _____ the gift
for the party? (hid   hide)

3. Does your new hat _____ ?
(fit   fight)

Reading and Thinking

1. Check the answer that tells what the story is mostly about.

_____ Uncle Bunny's supper

_____ how an owl uses its ears

_____ night sounds in the forest

Write **T** if the sentence is true.
Write **F** if it is not true.

2. _____ Uncle Bunny couldn't see
Cynthia's ears because she
didn't have any.

3. _____ Owls hear sounds from all
around because they turn
their heads almost around.

4. Check the sentence that tells how owls and rabbits are like each other.

_____ They both have ears.

_____ They both eat carrots.

_____ They both can fly.

Write **R** by the real things. Write **M** by the make-believe things.

5. _____ Owls can hear very well.

6. _____ Owls can hear clover grow.

7. _____ Owl ears can't be seen.

8. _____ Owls hear better than
rabbits.

The Red Coats Are Coming

Read this story to find out about two angry friends.

1 One morning as I was hopping to the meadow, I heard angry voices. I had to find out what was wrong.

2 I hopped toward the chattering. The voices got louder and louder. Soon I found two of my forest friends. They were shouting at each other.

3 "My red coat is the prettiest in the forest!" cried Biff the redbird. "It's made of feathers and it covers almost my whole body. It is soft and very pretty. Sometimes I go to the pond just to look at myself."

4 "Soft and pretty!" answered Mrs. Coats, the ladybug. "My coat is red, too, but it is shiny and has pretty little spots on it. Not only that, my red coat helps keep me safe."

5 I sat there and watched my two friends. Suddenly I had an idea.

6 "Stop!" I cried. "I've heard enough! My red coat is the best of all! It has bright buttons. One of my pockets is big enough to hold both of you. And if my coat gets old, I can throw it away and get a new one."

7 My two friends looked at each other. "Did we really sound that silly, Uncle Bunny?" asked Mrs. Coats.

8 "Maybe we should wait for something more important to argue about," Biff added.

9 "That is a good idea," I chuckled. "Now let's go and have lunch."

Knowing the Words

Write the words from the story that have these meanings.

1. all of something _____
(Par. 3)

2. having great
meaning _____
(Par. 8)

3. laughed quietly _____
(Par. 9)

In each row, circle the two words with opposite meanings.

4. start   right   wrong   begin

5. new   forest   trees   old

6. sound   noise   louder   quieter

7. there   here   now   time

Learning to Study

Write each group of words in A-B-C order. Each group of words will make a sentence. Use a period or a question mark to end each sentence.

1. move didn't wagon Barnie the

_____

_____

2. whistles new Children silver like

_____

_____

Reading and Thinking

1. Check the answer that tells what the story is mostly about.

_____ Biff's soft red feathers

_____ friends arguing about things that are not really important

_____ how Uncle Bunny gets a new red coat

Words such as *he, she,* and *it* take the place of other words. Read these sentences. Then fill in the blanks.

2. Biff smiled as he talked.

He stands for _____.

3. Mrs. Coats sang as she worked.

She stands for _____.

4. My coat is red, but it is shiny.

It stands for _____.

Too Late for Supper

Why did Uncle Bunny miss supper?

1   Sometimes I take a nap in the afternoon. I like to rest in the meadow where the sun is warm. I can count on Gordy Goldfinch to wake me for supper. Most times I have no trouble hearing him. But one time I slept right through his song.

2   That day my ears hurt. I had put cotton in them to keep them warm.

Then I hopped to the meadow to rest by the fence. Soon I was sound asleep. As I slept, I dreamed about the carrots I would have for supper.

3   Just before dark, Gordy flew to the meadow. He took his place on the fence as he always does. "Cheer-eee-ooo, cheer-eee-ooo, it's supper time for you," he sang.

4   I couldn't hear him. My ears were full of cotton. Gordy sang another song. Still I didn't move. The sun went down and I was still asleep. Gordy hopped down onto my head. Then he saw the cotton in my ears. He started pulling at the cotton.

5   "Rabbits crabbits!" I cried. "Who is wiggling my ears?"

6   "It's me, Uncle Bunny," Gordy answered. "I tried to wake you. I'm afraid you missed eating."

7   "Oh no, I haven't," I cried as I jumped up. "I may be too late for supper, but it's never too early for breakfast!"

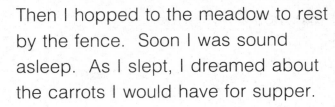

Knowing the Words

Check the meaning that fits the underlined word in each sentence.

1. Uncle Bunny likes to take a <u>rest</u> in the afternoon.

   _____ that which is left

   _____ time without work

2. The sun went down and I was <u>still</u> asleep.

   _____ quiet

   _____ up to this time

Working with Words

A word part that can be said by itself is called a **syllable.** Some words have two consonants between two vowels. These words can be divided between the consonants, as in *pic/nic.* In each word below, draw a line to divide the word into syllables.

1. c o t t o n   5. m o n k e y

2. a l w a y s   6. s i l l y

3. w i n d o w   7. c h i m n e y

4. a l m o s t   8. e n g i n e

Reading and Thinking

1. Check the answer that tells what the story is mostly about.

   _____ how Uncle Bunny hurt his ear

   _____ how Uncle Bunny slept through supper

   _____ Gordy's loud, clear singing voice

2. Check the two words that tell about Gordy.

   _____ friendly   _____ mean

   _____ tired   _____ helping

Write the best word to finish each sentence below.

3. The _____ needs to be painted again. (cotton, fence, word)

4. The new road is _____ and even. (wide, green, late)

5. The _____ made us feel much better. (dirt, engine, nap)

115

The Insect Eater

Who helps Uncle Bunny get some sleep?

1   Sometimes Brown Bat frightens people, but she really is a good friend.

2   One night I was asleep under a berry bush. Something brushed against my nose. When I tried to go back to sleep, it went zzz-zz-zzz in my ear. I wiggled my ear and turned over. I was almost asleep again when it bit my other ear.

3   This time I was wide awake and very angry. I thought to myself, "If that insect bothers me again, I'll be ready!" I lay down again and closed my eyes. I held my cane in one paw.

4   Soon I heard the buzz again. I got my cane ready. The sound got louder and louder. Whoosh! Something with wings and tiny sharp teeth flew past my face. The teeth closed. The zzz-zz-zzz was gone!

5   "Now you'll be able to sleep, Uncle Bunny," a voice said. The insect eater landed on a branch over my head. It hung upside down and folded its wings. It was Brown Bat.

6   "Thank you, Brown Bat," I said. "Could I give you some carrots as a thank you?"

7   "Thank you, Uncle Bunny," she said, "But I just eat insects. I was happy to help. Now have a good sleep!"

Knowing the Words

Write the words from the story that have these meanings.

1. touched lightly _____
   (Par. 2)

2. makes angry _____
   (Par. 3)

Check the meaning that fits the underlined word in each sentence.

3. Something with wings and tiny teeth flew <u>past</u> my face.

   _____ by

   _____ some time before

4. Uncle Bunny lost his <u>cane</u>.

   _____ plant for making sugar

   _____ stick for walking

Working with Words

Write a word from the story that can stand for each pair of words.

1. I will _____
   (Par. 3)

2. you will _____
   (Par. 5)

An 's shows that a thing belongs to someone. Change these words to show what belongs to someone.

3. bat _____ wings

4. Barnie _____ tail

Reading and Thinking

1. What animals were in the story?

   _____

   _____

2. What did the insect bite?

   _____

3. Brown Bat didn't want any

   carrots because _____

   _____.

Write **T** if the sentence is true.
Write **F** if it is not true.

4. _____ Uncle Bunny thinks bats are animals that help.

5. _____ Brown Bat eats apples.

6. _____ Uncle Bunny likes all insects.

Whistler Digs a Home

Would you like to live underground?

1   Whistler Woodchuck lives under the ground in a long tunnel. The front door is a hole. A large rock hides it. Whistler's living room is an open space in the tunnel. The tunnel has back doors and secret paths, too.

2   He is always working to make his house better. One day I heard digging and scratching under the large rock.

3   "What does he do with all the dirt?" I thought. I looked in his front door, but I couldn't see anything. The sounds were coming closer. I sat near the front door to wait for Whistler.

4   The minutes passed, but Whistler was still under the ground. I looked into the tunnel again. All at once a stream of dirt came flying out the door. My mouth, nose, and eyes were all filled with it.

5   "Bless my ears and—achoo!" I sneezed so hard I fell over onto my back. I sat up, wiped my face, and shook my ears. Then I saw Whistler.

6   He was backing out of his hole. He was still kicking dirt wildly behind him. That's when I learned how Whistler took the dirt out of his house. The next time I won't wait so close to the door.

Knowing the Words

Write the words from the story that have these meanings.

1. an open path
   under the ground _____
   (Par. 1)

2. something only
   a few know _____
   (Par. 1)

3. Check the meaning that fits the underlined word in the sentence.

   I sneezed so <u>hard</u> I fell over.

   _____ not easy to do

   _____ not soft

Learning to Study

To put words in A-B-C order you must first look at the first letter of each word. If the first letters are the same, look at the second letters. Number each list to show A-B-C order.

1. _____ nose   2. _____ sound

   _____ eyes   _____ sneezed

   _____ mouth   _____ stream

   _____ face   _____ scratch

Reading and Thinking

1. Check the answer that tells what the story is mostly about.

   _____ finding the secret tunnel

   _____ Uncle Bunny's dirty face

   _____ Whistler digging a tunnel

2. Number the sentences to show what happened first, second, third, and last.

   _____ Uncle Bunny heard digging and scratching.

   _____ Uncle Bunny got his face full of dirt.

   _____ Uncle Bunny sat down to wait for Whistler.

   _____ Uncle Bunny fell over onto his back.

Write **T** if the sentence is true.
Write **F** if it is not true.

3. _____ A woodchuck's home is dark.

4. _____ A woodchuck needs strong paws.

5. What do you think Uncle Bunny will do the next time he sees Whistler digging a tunnel?

   _____

A Hard Day's Work

Read about a small worker who is very strong.

1 "Hello, Uncle Bunny," a tired voice said to me one morning. I was on my way to the carrot patch for a quick breakfast. I looked around, but I didn't see anyone.

2 "Down here, Uncle Bunny," the voice went on. "I'm down here!" I looked toward the sound. There wasn't anyone in sight. "Please don't step on me," the little voice called.

3 I looked again. This time I saw a small seed moving across the path. But a seed had never talked to me.

4 I stretched out on the ground to get a closer look. That's when I found the answer. The talking seed was really Cookie Ant. Cookie is so tiny that the seed covered his whole body.

5 "Cookie!" I exclaimed. "That seed is ten times bigger than you are! How can you carry it?"

6 "It's hard work, Uncle Bunny," he replied. "But lots of ants carry even bigger things. We all work to keep our little ant town going. Some of us find food. Some of us take care of our home. Some of us do other things to help."

7 "Bless my ears and whiskers!" I exclaimed. "That sounds like a good idea. Maybe rabbits should start living like ants."

Knowing the Words

Write the words from the story that have these meanings.

1. reached across _____
   (Par. 4)

2. small insects _____
   (Par. 6)

Words that mean the same or nearly the same are called **synonyms.** Circle two synonyms in each row.

3. body   tiny   small   seed

4. toward   sound   away   noise

5. begin   read   answers   start

Working with Words

Write the best word to finish each sentence below.

1. I _____ the answer. (wrote, rope, rode)

2. You took the _____ street. (rock, rest, wrong)

When **un-** is added to a word, it changes the meaning of the word. The word part **un-** means "not." *Unreal* means "not real." Add **un-** to these words to finish the sentences.

3. She was _____hurt in the fall.

4. The food was _____touched.

Reading and Thinking

1. Check the answer that tells what the story is mostly about.

   _____ Uncle Bunny learning about how ants work

   _____ seeds that walk and talk at the same time

   _____ how Cookie Ant became so strong

2. How big was the seed that

   Cookie was carrying? _____

   _____

3. How was Cookie helping the ant

   town? _____

   _____

Write the best word to finish each sentence below.

4. The train went through the

   _____ under the river. (mud, tunnel, water)

5. I _____ my hair before I left for school. (brushed, learned, practiced)

6. Take the dishes _____ the kitchen. (under, above, into)

Chomper's Treasure

What could a chipmunk do with a big ear of corn?

1   One day last fall I was crossing a field. Suddenly a brown streak with white and black stripes hurried between my legs. "Bless my ears and whiskers!" I cried. "I've never seen lightning with stripes before!"

2   The streak came to a stop on the road. I saw that it was really Chomper Chipmunk. He had stopped beside an ear of corn bigger than he was.

3   "Look what I found, Uncle Bunny!" Chomper cried. "I've got to carry it away before the crows find it."

4   He bit the pieces of corn off the ear one by one. Then he filled his cheeks with the corn. Chomper's face got fatter and fatter until it was the widest part of his body. When there was no more room in his cheeks, he hurried away. He dropped into his house through a small hole under a rock.

5   Soon Chomper ran back to the corn. He filled his cheeks again and ran off. He made the same trip again and again until all the corn was gone.

6   "Chomper," I said, "you put away a lot of corn. You sleep most of the winter. Why do you need so much food?"

7   "I do sleep a lot," he answered. "But my dreams make me very hungry before spring!"

Knowing the Words

Write the words from the story that have these meanings.

1. sides of the face under the eyes _____
(Par. 4)

2. wanting food _____
(Par. 7)

Circle the three words in each row that belong together.

3. nap   dream   sight   sleep

4. fly   chipmunk   mouse   squirrel

5. ran   hurried   scampered   sat

Working with Words

Write the best word to finish each sentence below.

1. Do you _____ the new teacher? (know, nose, noise)

2. Did someone _____ on the door? (nest, lock, knock)

Write these compound words beside their meanings.

underground   sunset   afternoon

3. when sun goes down _____

4. later than noon _____

5. under the ground _____

Reading and Thinking

1. What color were Chomper's stripes? _____

2. Check two sentences that show Chomper was smaller than Uncle Bunny.

_____ Chomper ran between Uncle Bunny's legs.

_____ The ear of corn was bigger than Chomper.

_____ Chomper's cheeks got very fat.

3. How are crows like chipmunks?

_____

Write **R** by the real things. Write **M** by the make-believe things.

4. _____ Lightning had lunch with Uncle Bunny.

5. _____ Chipmunks put away food for the winter.

6. _____ Chipmunks can carry lots of food in their cheeks.

A Place to Hide

Animals have different ways to keep safe. Read to find out what the bobwhites do to keep safe.

1 "How is the biggest family in the meadow?" I called. The Bobwhites had all their children out in the field that evening.

2 "We're fine, Uncle Bunny," Mr. Bobwhite said. "Would you like to join us? We are having our evening hiding lessons."

3 "Thank you, Mr. Bobwhite," I said. "That sounds like fun!" Soon I found an open place to watch the babies. They looked like balls of fuzz with legs.

4 "Now children," Mrs. Bobwhite said. "Pretend a hawk is near and you need to hide." At once all the bobwhites were gone.

5 "Ah-bob-white!" Mrs. Bobwhite called. Babies came from their hiding places like magic.

6 "It's time for bed," said Mr. Bobwhite. "Let's make our sleeping circle." The birds moved close to him while Mrs. Bobwhite counted heads.

7 "Oh dear," she said, "there are only fifteen. Where's Peter?"

8 "I'm over here!" a little voice said. The voice came from my coat.

9 I pulled my paw out of my pocket. A little head popped out. "Bless my ears and whiskers!" I said. "Peter found the best hiding place of all!"

Knowing the Words

Write the words from the story that have these meanings.

1. things to learn _____
   (Par. 2)

2. play make-believe _____
   (Par. 4)

3. made a short,
   quick move
   or sound _____
   (Par. 9)

Circle the three words in each row that belong together.

4. watch   look   hide   see

5. hawk   deer   bobwhite   crow

Working with Words

In each sentence, circle three words with the same vowel sound as the word in dark print.

1. **now**   The cow found the sweet grass and gave a loud MOO!

2. **now**   How can I drive around the mountain?

Reading and Thinking

1. Check the answer that tells what the story is mostly about.

   _____ a circle of sleeping birds

   _____ hiding lessons for the bobwhite babies

   _____ counting bobwhite babies

2. How many babies do Mr. and Mrs. Bobwhite have? _____

3. What did the bobwhite babies pretend? _____

   _____

Write **T** if the sentence is true.
Write **F** if it is not true.

4. _____ Bobwhites sleep in trees.

5. _____ Uncle Bunny's coat talks.

6. _____ Bobwhites are afraid of hawks.

7. Check two words that tell about Peter Bobwhite.

   _____ large

   _____ fuzzy

   _____ clever

Bumbles Finds a Friend

What does it mean to be a friend?

1 I had just found a cool place for my nap. I put one paw over my eyes and thought about a spring clover field. But I couldn't go to sleep.

2 Somewhere close by someone was crying. I waited a few minutes, but the cries just got louder.

3 "Bless my ears and whiskers! I can't sleep with this noise," I thought. So I got up, brushed my whiskers, and went to see about it.

4 I found Bumbles with big tears running down his face. "Oh, Uncle Bunny, I'm so unhappy. I can't do anything right! I'm always breaking things or running into someone. No one will even come close to me!"

5 Bumbles sneezed. His head flew up and knocked my glasses off. "See what I mean?" he cried.

6 Prickles came walking by. She saw Bumbles crying and stopped. "I don't have any friends," Bumbles said to Prickles. "I'm so unhappy!"

7 "Look at me, Bumbles," Prickles said. "I have these sharp things all over me. Nobody wants to get very close to me either. Maybe we can help each other."

8 "Uncle Bunny," Bumbles said, "I'm starting to feel better now. I'd like you to meet my new friend Prickles."

Knowing the Words

In each row, circle two words that have opposite meanings.

1. see   close   far   look
2. never   few   always   some
3. cry   break   sleep   wake

Working with Words

A word part that can be said by itself is called a **syllable.** Some words have two consonants between two vowels. These words can be divided between the consonants, as in *pic/nic.* In each word below, draw a line to divide the word into syllables.

1. h a p p y   3. w o n d e r
2. w h i s p e r   4. t r a c t o r

Walk and *talk* are **rhyming words.** In rhyming words, only the beginning sound is different. Write words that rhyme with *spring* by changing *spr* in *spring* to *r* or *w.*

5. _____   6. _____

Then use each new word in the right sentence.

7. The bird hurt its _____.

8. Will the school bell _____?

Reading and Thinking

1. Check the answer that tells what the story is mostly about.

    _____ Uncle Bunny's glasses

    _____ sleeping with noise

    _____ finding a friend

Write the best word to finish each sentence below.

2. If you _____ the toy, you must fix it. (jump, break, cry)

3. The _____ of the train kept us awake. (noise, rain, floating)

4. Move _____ to the front so you can see better. (later, closer, wider)

Read these sentences. Then fill in the blanks.

5. Bumbles sneezed as he cried.

    He stands for _____.

6. Prickles saw me as she walked by.

    She stands for _____.

7. The cane slipped as it hit the ice.

    It stands for _____.

A Road for Mice

Why do you think Chubby Meadow Mouse would want a straight road?

1   One morning I was hopping through the meadow. I caught my toe on a stone and hit the ground. "Rabbits crabbits!" I shouted as I pulled myself to my knees. "Stone, why don't you keep out of the way?"

2   Just then I heard tiny footsteps coming toward me. I looked up. There was Chubby Meadow Mouse looking right at me.

3   "You fell so hard, Uncle Bunny," he said. "The ground shook! Are you hurt?"

4   "My bones are shaken and my fur is dirty," I answered, "but I'm all right. That stone tripped me!"

5   "We have been trying to move that stone for a very long time," Chubby said. "We had to build our road around it. Maybe we can push it out of the way now."

6   We pushed and pulled with all our might. First the stone wiggled one way, then the other way. At last it rolled away into the grass.

7   "Thank you, Uncle Bunny," Chubby said. "Now we can make our road straight. We don't like to slow down for curves in the road when we are being chased!"

8   "I am happy to help," I said. "Maybe some day you can help me build a road straight to the clover field!"

128

Knowing the Words

Words that mean the same or nearly the same are called **synonyms.** Circle two synonyms in each row.

1. dirty   rock   stone   clean

2. road   path   knees   toes

3. straight   curves   looked   saw

Working with Words

Words that end in *s, ss, x, sh,* or *ch* add **-es** to show more than one. Rewrite these words to show more than one. One is done for you.

dress ___*dresses*___

1. box _____

2. pass _____

3. flash _____

Circle the right word to finish each sentence. Then write the word in the blank.

4. We _____ bikes through the forest.   (rod   rode)

5. The car slipped on the _____.   (is   ice)

6. Most mornings I _____ to the carrot patch.   (hop   hope)

Reading and Thinking

1. Number the sentences to show what happened first, second, third, and last.

   _____ Uncle Bunny and Chubby pushed and pulled a stone.

   _____ The stone rolled away into the grass.

   _____ Chubby thanked Uncle Bunny for his help.

   _____ Uncle Bunny fell down.

2. Because a stone was in the way, the mice couldn't _____

   _____.

Write **T** if the sentence is true.
Write **F** if it is not true.

3. _____ Chubby can run faster on straight roads.

4. _____ The road was already straight.

5. _____ The stone was heavy.

6. The next time Uncle Bunny hops through the meadow, he may

   _____

   _____.

Dropping In on Musky

What happens when Uncle Bunny sees something he doesn't know about?

1 "Bless my ears and whiskers!" I said. "I don't remember that island in the middle of the stream. It looks like a pile of grass and weeds."

2 The longer I looked, the more I wondered. Then I told myself, "Uncle Bunny, you won't find out anything by watching and wondering." I took a deep breath. I got a running start. I made a big leap and fell right through the top of the island.

3 A voice under me said, "If you are not a dream, please get up. If you are a dream, please let me wake up." I stood up and a sleepy muskrat sat up and stretched.

4 "I didn't know this was someone's house," I said. "I thought it was an island. I'm sorry I fell through your roof and on top of you!"

5 "Oh, it's you, Uncle Bunny!" said Musky. "Don't worry about the roof. I can fix it with mud and weeds."

6 "Well, you do have a different kind of house," I said. "How do you get in and out?"

7 "Over here," Musky said. She showed me a tunnel under the water.

8 "If it's OK with you, I think I should leave the way I came in," I said. "If I used your door, my ears would get so full of water they would not stand up straight!"

130

Knowing the Words

Check the meaning that fits the underlined word in each sentence.

1. Did she <u>run</u> in the race?

   _____ move fast on legs

   _____ what a machine does

2. The tree needs a <u>deep</u> hole.

   _____ having a low voice

   _____ a long way to the bottom

3. The children <u>watch</u> the puppy.

   _____ small clock

   _____ look at

Learning to Study

To put words in A-B-C order you must first look at the first letter of each word. If the first letters are the same, look at the second letters. Number each list to show A-B-C order.

1. _____ stood   3. _____ muskrat

   _____ sleepy   _____ minute

   _____ secret   _____ acorn

   _____ safe   _____ maybe

2. _____ deep   4. _____ wonder

   _____ island   _____ leap

   _____ bless   _____ weeds

   _____ set   _____ wheel

Reading and Thinking

Use the groups of words in the box to finish the sentences below.

- it looked like a pile of weeds
- he could fix it
- he wanted to see what was there

1. Uncle Bunny jumped on the

   island because _____

   _____.

2. Uncle Bunny thought Musky's

   house was an island because ____

   _____.

3. Musky wasn't angry about his

   roof because _____

   _____.

Glenda Gives a Gift

Would you like to have Glenda Goat for a friend? Why or why not?

1   Glenda Goat is always busy. She wants to climb and stand on top of everything. If there is a hill or a rock or a log nearby, Glenda will be standing on it.

2   One afternoon, I leaned against an old log to rest in the warm sun. All at once my face felt cold. Above me everything grew dark. I opened my eyes and looked up. There was Glenda, blocking the sun.

3   "Were you asleep?" Glenda asked. Before I could answer, she said, "I need your help. I need to find a gift for my best friend. Do you have any ideas?"

4   "The best gift," I said, "is a gift just for that friend. You could write and sing a special song. A song would be a wonderful gift to give."

5   "If I sing," Glenda said, laughing, "my friend won't want to be my friend anymore!"

6   Then I had an idea. "What do you like to eat?" I asked.

7   "Small plants and grass are my favorites," Glenda answered.

8   "If your friend has a yard," I said, "you could cut the grass for her by chewing it." So Glenda found the perfect gift. She could do something special for her friend and have fun, too.

Knowing the Words

Write the words from the story that have these meanings.

1. a present _____
(Par. 3)

2. with nothing wrong _____
(Par. 8)

Working with Words

Circle the right word to finish each sentence. Then write the word in the blank.

1. The snow is always _____.

(cold   fold)

2. He got a new milk _____.

(cut   cup)

When a word ends in *e*, the *e* may be dropped before adding **-ed** or **-ing**. Add **-ing** to these words. Then use the new words in the sentences below. One is done for you.

bounce + ing *bouncing*

3. leave + ing _____

4. He is _____ the cane beside the tree.

5. I am _____ a ball up and down.

Reading and Thinking

1. Check the answer that tells what the story is mostly about.

_____ finding the right gift

_____ standing on hills or rocks

_____ Uncle Bunny's nap

Write the best word to finish each sentence.

2. The right gift will make someone

very _____.
(happy, lost, flat)

3. Please _____ the grass.
(read, open, cut)

4. Check the group of words that tells about Glenda.

_____ a very good singer

_____ thinking of others

_____ not a good friend

133

Molly Gets a Scare

Have you ever learned a lesson from being scared?

1   One day at the stream I saw my friend Donna Duck. She was giving swimming lessons to her little ducks. Five little ducks followed close behind her. Donna called, "Right foot first, then left foot. Try not to splash. Paddle smoothly, and wiggle your tail once in a while."

2   "Hi, Uncle Bunny," Donna called. She and her duck parade swam past.

3   "Hello, ducks," I answered. All the ducks waved to me in turn as they swam by me.

4   "Hi, Uncle Furry Ears!" a voice called. Far behind was the last little duck. It was Molly, splashing and throwing water everywhere.

5   "Molly," Donna cried, "his name is Uncle Bunny! Now stop being silly and catch up with us!"

6   Molly caught up. The little duck parade went on. But soon Molly was off again, this time after a flower.

7   "Maybe I can help," I said to Donna. I sat down behind a bush to wait for Molly. "Oogly-boogly, rabbits crabbits!" I shouted in my loudest voice.

8   "Help! Help!" Molly cried as she splashed toward Donna. I guess that scare was enough for Molly. Now she's always first in the duck parade!

Knowing the Words

Write the words from the story that have these meanings.

1. move the feet in water _____
   (Par. 1)

2. evenly _____
   (Par. 1)

3. did swim _____
   (Par. 2)

In each row, circle the two words with opposite meanings.

4. close   tiny   far   little

5. soap   last   first   mud

6. smooth   loudest   softest   gone

Working with Words

The ending **-er** means "more," so *prouder* means "more proud." The ending **-est** means "most," so *proudest* means "most proud." Add the endings **-er** and **-est** to these base words. One is done for you.

Joe is the tall*est* of six boys.

1. Donna is old_____ than Molly.

2. I was the loud_____ of the four.

Reading and Thinking

1. Write two things ducks must do to swim well.

   _____

   _____

Write **T** if the sentence is true.
Write **F** if it is not true.

2. _____ Molly was a playful duck.

3. _____ Uncle Bunny wanted to help.

4. _____ Donna Duck taught her children not to be silly.

5. _____ Ducks are always afraid of rabbits.

6. _____ Baby ducks always know how to swim.

7. Molly was scared because _____

   _____.

Write the best word to finish each sentence.

8. Judy _____ the keys in the basket.
   (splashed, hid, woke)

9. The girl _____ her hand to show she was ready.
   (washed, bit, waved)

The Shy Singer

Read the story to find out why Uncle Bunny can't sleep.

1 One summer night I was asleep under a bush. All at once I was so startled I almost jumped out of my fur! Just then another long, loud "Gah-ROM, gah-ROM!" came from the stream close by. This time I knew the sound was Mr. Bullfrog.

2 First I tried to cover my ears. That didn't help. Then I rolled them up. Still the noise pushed through. The sound went on through the night. I began to wish I had no ears at all!

3 The next morning I went to visit Mr. Bullfrog. He was sitting on a log in the stream, catching insects. "Mr. Bullfrog," I shouted, "I heard lots of loud noise coming from here last night."

4 "That wasn't noise, Uncle Bunny," he said. "That was singing." And he put out his tongue to catch a fly.

5 "Well, your voice is so loud and deep it keeps me awake," I said. "Why don't you sing in the daytime?"

6 "I'm sorry, Uncle Bunny," he said. "I'm too shy to sing in the daytime. I was singing a love song to the lady frogs."

7 "Maybe the lady frogs like his singing," I thought. "As for me, I'll be glad when summer is over. Then Mr. Bullfrog will stop singing, and I can start sleeping!"

Knowing the Words

Write the words from the story that have these meanings.

1. surprised _____
   (Par. 1)

2. part of a tree _____
   (Par. 3)

3. part of
   the mouth _____
   (Par. 4)

Check the meaning that fits the underlined word in each sentence.

4. Does a fly have wings?

   _____ insect

   _____ move in the air

5. I'm glad the show is over.

   _____ on the other side

   _____ done, finished

6. My ears hurt from the noise.

   _____ parts of corn plants

   _____ things used for hearing

Learning to Study

Number the words to show A-B-C order for each list.

1. _____ shy   2. _____ log

   _____ here   _____ lady

   _____ startled   _____ glad

   _____ loud   _____ like

Reading and Thinking

1. Number the sentences to show what happened first, second, third, and last.

   _____ Uncle Bunny visited Mr. Bullfrog.

   _____ Uncle Bunny heard a noise.

   _____ Mr. Bullfrog told why he sings at night.

   _____ Uncle Bunny was asleep.

2. Check two answers that tell how Mr. Bullfrog's tongue is like yours.

   _____ He uses it to eat.

   _____ He catches flies with it.

   _____ He uses it to talk.

Write **R** by the real things. Write **M** by the make-believe things.

3. _____ Frogs can make noises.

4. _____ Rabbits can jump out of their fur.

Write the best word to finish each sentence below.

5. A frog's _____ is very long. (tongue, dress, car)

6. Uncle Bunny likes to _____ at night. (sleep, bark, fly)

Growing Up

How do animals and people change as they grow up?

1   One morning I was on my way to the carrot patch. Suddenly I saw a spot of bright color in the sky. I watched and saw the spot move. Slowly it got larger. Then I knew the spot was coming closer.

2   The bright spot turned out to be my little friend Angel Butterfly. "Angel," I called, "your wings are so bright in the sun! It's fun to watch you fly. Flying must be a wonderful way to move around!"

3   "Yes, Uncle Bunny," Angel replied, "I do like to fly! I can see so many things from up in the air. And I can move lots faster, too."

4   "Sometimes I think I would like to fly," I chuckled. "Somehow my paws just won't work like wings!"

5   "I wasn't always like this," Angel said. "I used to have to crawl on tiny little legs. Even moving from one plant to another was hard. When winter came, I built my little house to keep me safe. In the spring I woke up like this."

6   "That is called growing up," I said. "Some of us change a lot, the way you did. Some of us just become a different size. I used to be a little bunny. Now I'm just bigger."

7   "Growing up is fun, Uncle Bunny," Angel said. "I'm glad I learned to fly."

Knowing the Words

Words that mean the same or nearly the same are called **synonyms.** In each row below, circle the two words that are synonyms.

1. closer   in   out   nearer

2. fly   see   look   sky

In each row, circle the two words with opposite meanings.

3. came   slowly   quickly   saw

4. always   sometimes   many   few

5. yes   no   things   always

Working with Words

Write the best word to finish each sentence below.

1. Angel likes to _____.
(fly, try, cry)

2. _____ is the best part of the year. (Spring, Thing, String)

Fill in each blank with the right pair of letters to make a word.

ar   or   ur

3. The little bunny grew l_____ge.

4. I ate this m_____ning.

5. We t_____ned the page to read.

Reading and Thinking

1. Put a check by two words that tell about Angel Butterfly.

____ happy   ____ crawling

____ angry   ____ flying

2. Look at the picture. Check the two sentences that tell about it.

____ Uncle Bunny is eating the carrot.

____ Uncle Bunny ate the carrot.

____ Angel is flying.

Write the best word to finish each sentence.

3. The small plant _____ larger. (moved, came, grew)

4. My coat keeps me _____.
(little, warm, friendly)

Nibbler Makes a Mistake

Find out about Nibbler's mistake and what he can do to fix it.

1 Bonnie Beaver and her grandson Nibbler live in the stream. They have a house made of sticks and mud. Bonnie made a dam to hold back the water and to make a safe place for her family.

2 One day I heard Bonnie talking to Nibbler. "Don't forget," she said, "trees have leaves, but fence posts don't. Don't chew on any more fence posts. Cut down a little tree. We can use it to fix our house."

3 I leaned back on my cane to watch. Bonnie sat up on her back legs. She started to work on a tree with her sharp teeth. She took big bites until she had made a deep cut on one side. I watched and waited for the tree to fall.

4 Crack! Something broke, but not the tree! I felt myself falling. Then I hit the ground. Nibbler had cut down my cane! He thought it was a small tree.

5 "Oh, Uncle Bunny, I'm very sorry!" Nibbler said. "I thought your ears were the leaves."

6 Just then Bonnie's tree fell across the stream. "I've got an idea, Uncle Bunny!" Nibbler shouted. "I'll make you a new cane from that tree."

7 Now each time I use my beautiful new cane I think of the day Nibbler made a mistake.

Knowing the Words

Write the words from the story that have these meanings.

1. wall to hold
   back water _____
   (Par. 1)

2. something
   done wrong _____
   (Par. 7)

Working with Words

Write the best word to finish each sentence below.

1. Storms can bring _____.
   (rain, ran, run)

2. Can you _____ the new word?
   (said, sad, say)

3. I _____ the answer.
   (now, know, not)

An 's at the end of a word shows that a thing belongs to someone or something. Change these groups of words by using 's.

4. the branch of the tree

   the _____ branch

5. the home of Bonnie

   _____ home

Reading and Thinking

1. What did Bonnie Beaver build in the stream near her home?

   _____

2. Check the answer that tells what the story is mostly about.

   _____ how beavers chew on
         fence posts

   _____ beavers cutting down trees

   _____ how to build a dam

3. Check two sentences that tell how Bonnie could use the tree she cut.

   _____ She could use the branches
         to fix her house.

   _____ She could use the tree for
         fence posts.

   _____ She could use the tree to
         make the dam stronger.

4. Check two words about Nibbler.

   _____ sorry   _____ angry

   _____ mixed-up   _____ excited

141

The Shortcut

How might Uncle Bunny get across the pond?

1   For some reason carrots just didn't sound good to me one morning. Clover seemed like a much better breakfast. Not long ago I had seen some fresh, new clover across the pond. I could almost taste the clover as I thought about it.

2   Just then Sal Swan sailed along. She was looking for water plants. "Good morning, Sal," I said. "Who is your little friend?" Sal had one of her babies riding on her wide back.

3   "Hello, Uncle Bunny," Sal answered. "This is Sandy."

4   "What a fine way to look for your breakfast!" I said. Sandy just looked back at me and smiled.

5   "What are you doing here, Uncle Bunny?" Sal asked. "I thought you would be at the carrot patch."

6   "This morning I just didn't feel like eating carrots," I said. "I can't help thinking about the new clover field across the pond."

7   "Would you like a ride?" Sal asked. "That is, if you don't mind a friend." So I climbed on Sal's back and had a quick trip across the pond.

8   "I'm afraid you'll have to walk back, Uncle Bunny," Sal said. "By then you'll have a breakfast of fresh clover."

Reading and Thinking

1. Check the answer that tells what the story is mostly about.

   _____ how swans swim

   _____ how Uncle Bunny goes across the pond

   _____ eating carrots for breakfast

Read these sentences. Then fill in the blanks.

2. Sandy wiggled as she cleaned her feathers.

   She stands for _____.

3. The clover leaned as it grew.

   It stands for _____.

4. Sal swam as she washed.

   She stands for _____.

Working with Words

Write the best word to finish each sentence below.

1. I have a _____ on my dress. (pen, pine, pin)

2. Can you _____ the horse? (ride, red, roll)

3. That book is _____. (win, mine, men)

4. Will you feed the _____? (can, car, cat)

5. The boys _____ their lunch. (cook, look, book)

When **re-** is added to a word, it changes the meaning of the word. The word part **re-** means "again." *Refill* means "fill again." Add **re-** to these words to finish the sentences.

6. I will _____build the house.

7. Who will _____do these papers?

8. Please _____fill the tall jar.

9. Did you _____write the test?

10. Did the station _____run the show?

11. Please _____tell the story.

Sunny to the Rescue

Read about how Sunny helps Uncle Bunny.

1   Today was the day to comb my whiskers. I hopped to a quiet pool near the edge of the stream. The water was very still. I could see my face looking back at me.

2   I pulled a small branch from a pine tree to use as a comb. Then I leaned over the water. A streak of colors flashed before my eyes. "Bless my ears and whiskers!" I cried, leaning over a little farther.

3   All at once something splashed into the water. Then everything looked fuzzy. My glasses had fallen off my nose. They were resting on the bottom of the stream!

4   Then I heard a voice from under the water. "Who is dropping things into my home? I'm trying to keep eggs safe."

5   "I'm sorry to bother you," I said. "I dropped my glasses."

6   "Oh, it's you, Uncle Bunny," Sunny Sunfish said as he swam toward me. "The water isn't deep here. If you reach down, I think I can move your glasses into your paw."

7   I dipped both paws into the water. Sunny pushed with his nose, and soon I was holding my glasses. "Thank you, Sunny," I said. "From now on I'll comb my whiskers over a puddle!"

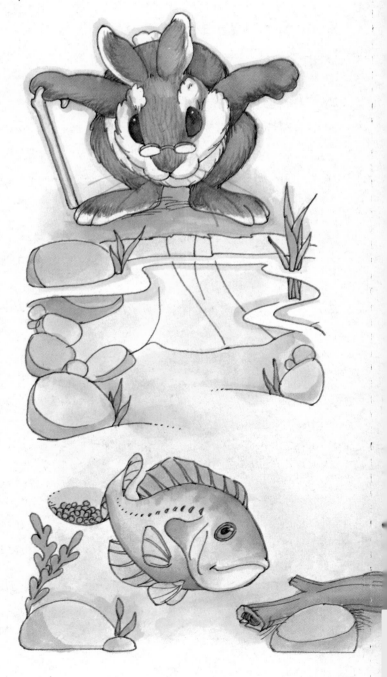

144

Write a compound word for the underlined words in each sentence.

1. A <u>storm</u> that brings <u>snow</u> is a

_____.

2. A game with a <u>ball</u> and <u>basket</u> is

_____.

Write the best word to finish each sentence below.

3. Be sure to look over _____ answer. (each   ears)

4. Uncle Bunny hid under a _____. (burn   bush)

5. I'll soon be in _____ grade. (word   third)

6. _____ to do your best. (Try   Fry)

1. Number the sentences to show what happened first, second, third, and last.

_____ Uncle Bunny's glasses fell.

_____ Sunny found the glasses.

_____ Sunny pushed the glasses.

_____ Uncle Bunny hopped to the pool.

Write the best word to finish each sentence.

2. The child took the _____ puppy for a walk. (deep, little, clover)

3. Can you see your _____ in the glass? (family, idea, face)

Look at the picture with the story. Write the best word to finish each sentence about the picture.

4. There is a _____ in the pool. (school, log, cage)

5. _____ are growing at the bottom of the pool. (Flowers, Rabbits, Plants)

6. The water is _____. (dirty, clean, moving)

145

A New Face at the Pond

How do you think Uncle Bunny might welcome someone new?

1 One evening I was going to the clover field across the pond. Someone I had not seen before was out on the water. The visitor looked like Sal Swan, but she had colored feathers. This bird was mostly gray and brown with some white. She had a long black neck and head. She looked a little like Donna Duck, but she was much larger.

2 I hopped around the pond. She came closer to me. "Hello," I said. "My name is Uncle Bunny. I don't think I've seen you here before."

3 "I'm happy to meet you, Uncle Bunny," she said. "I'm Greta Goose. Some friends and I are on our way back to our summer home."

4 "You mean you live in different places in summer and winter?" I asked. "That's a lot of moving!"

5 "We really like our summer home," she said. "But it gets too cold for us in the winter."

6 "Many of my friends sleep most of the winter," I said. "That keeps them safe from the cold."

7 "I don't think I would like to stay in bed all winter," Greta said. "All of us fly together and help each other. We have a lot of fun."

8 "It's good to learn how others live," I replied. "But I think I'll just stay here with my forest friends."

Knowing the Words

In each row, circle the two words with opposite meanings.

1. same   cold   cool   different
2. lake   long   short   pond

Working with Words

Walk and *talk* are **rhyming words.** In rhyming words, only the beginning sound is different. The missing words below rhyme with *shook*. Change *sh* in *shook* to *l, b, c,* and *t.* Then write each new word in the right sentence.

1. _____   3. _____

2. _____   4. _____

5. We _____ the wrong road.

6. Did you read the _____ ?

7. I can _____ dinner.

8. Did the car _____ new?

Write the best word to finish each sentence below.

9. I have not _____ her before. (send   seen)

10. We rode the _____ to school. (bone   bus)

Reading and Thinking

1. Check the answer that tells what the story is mostly about.

   _____ where Uncle Bunny is having dinner

   _____ meeting a new bird

   _____ Greta's safe trip

Read these sentences. Then fill in the blanks.

2. The stream sparkled as it splashed.

   It stands for _____ .

3. Sal swam as she talked to Uncle Bunny. *She* stands for _____ .

Write the best word to finish each sentence below.

4. The friends _____ letters at camp. (tell, write, do)

5. Some animals _____ berries. (make, buy, eat)

6. Did you _____ the milk? (stay, drink, grow)

7. What may Greta do after Uncle Bunny leaves? _____

   _____

A Slip on a Slide

Look at the picture. Why do you think Uncle Bunny is unhappy?

1 Susie Otter uses the stream as her playground. Her favorite thing is sliding in the mud. I was hopping along the bank one day when I heard a loud splash. I hurried ahead and saw Susie. She was scrambling out of the water. She shook herself. Water flew everywhere, even all over me.

2 "Oh, I'm sorry, Uncle Bunny," she said when she saw me. "I didn't know you were here. I just made a new slide. Would you like to try it?"

3 "It looks like fun, but I feel cold when I get wet," I replied. "How did you make the slide so smooth?"

4 "I had to move a lot of stones," Susie said, "and many plants and small branches. I've been working all week. There was one big rock stuck in the bank over there."

5 I hopped to the edge of her slide. I leaned over to see where the rock had been. My cane went one way and my feet went the other way. The next thing I knew I was at the bottom of Susie's slide, wet from ears to tail.

6 "Maybe we could call you Uncle Bunny Otter!" Susie laughed. "Aren't you glad you tried my new slide?"

7 "Rabbits crabbits!" I said, as the water ran down my whiskers. "I would like your slide better if it ended in the carrot patch!"

Knowing the Words

Circle the three words in each row that belong together.

1. water   stream   rock   pond
2. drive   slip   slide   fall
3. rocks   mud   stones   stuck
4. he   she   it   rabbit

Working with Words

Write the best word to finish each sentence below.

1. The class will _____ for the bird. (care   car)

2. Did someone _____ dinner? (barn   burn)

Most words add **-s** or **-es** to show more than one. Words that end in *y* are different. In most words that end in *y*, change the *y* to *i*, and add **-es.** Change the words below to mean more than one. One is done for you.
berry   *berries*

3. story _____

4. penny _____

5. puppy _____

6. library _____

Reading and Thinking

1. Check the answer that tells what the story is mostly about.

   _____ how Susie moved a rock from the bank

   _____ Uncle Bunny's wet whiskers

   _____ Susie Otter's new mud slide

2. How long did Susie work to make her slide? _____

3. Susie said she was sorry to Uncle Bunny because _____

   _____

4. Why doesn't Uncle Bunny like to get wet? _____

   _____

5. Check three sentences that tell how Susie Otter is a hard worker.

   _____ Susie moved one big rock from the bank.

   _____ Susie moved plants and branches.

   _____ Susie went down the slide.

   _____ Susie shook water all over.

   _____ Susie moved lots of stones to make her new slide.

Lefty's Old Suit

What do you do with clothes you can't wear anymore? Find out what one animal does.

1 The stream is one of my favorite places. It's a wonderful place for a treasure hunt. Sometimes I find a shiny stone or a pretty shell there. It's just fun to see what I can find.

2 One day I found an old suit that belonged to Lefty Crayfish. The thin shell was shaped just like Lefty. It looked as if he had been covered with ice but had crawled out of it.

3 "What could have happened to the rest of Lefty?" I thought. Then I saw his left front claw sticking out from under a rock. He had lost his right claw in a fight with another crayfish. Lefty is growing a new claw. It will soon be as big as the claw he lost, but we'll still call him Lefty.

4 "Lefty," I called, "I found the suit you lost!"

5 "Oh, I didn't lose it, Uncle Bunny," he said from under his rock. "That suit was too small. I pulled myself together and backed out of it. I'm growing a new suit, so I don't need the old one."

6 "Can you come out and show me your new suit?" I asked.

7 "My shell is still soft," Lefty answered. "It isn't safe for me to come out until it is hard."

8 "I'm glad I don't change my suit," I thought. "I would feel very strange hiding under a rock to grow new fur."

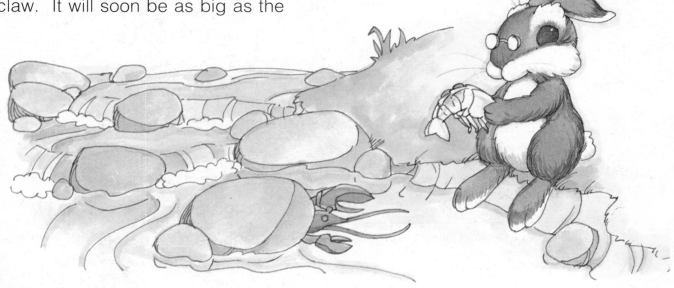

Knowing the Words

Circle two synonyms in each row.

1. glad   claw   stone   happy
2. lost   knew   rock   stone

Working with Words

The spelling of some base words is changed before an ending is added. Words such as *bat* must have the last letter doubled before adding **-ed** or **-ing.** Double the last letter and add the endings to these words to finish the sentences. One is done for you.

cut   hit   pet

(ed)   The dog likes to be *petted*

1. (ing) We are _____ the ball.

2. (ing) He is _____ the cake.

Circle the right word to finish the sentence. Then write the word in the blank.

3. Did you read the _____ ?
   (nine, sign, fine)

4. I heard what he _____.
   (said, fed, bed)

5. Please get the key to the _____.
   (cap, car, can)

Reading and Thinking

1. Check the answer that tells what the story is mostly about.

   _____ Lefty's missing claw

   _____ a crayfish's shell

   _____ a rock in the stream

2. What did Lefty's shell look like?

   _____

3. Uncle Bunny knew Lefty was

   under the rock because _____

   _____.

4. Why is Lefty called Lefty?

   _____

   _____

Write **T** if the sentence is true.
Write **F** if it is not true.

5. _____ Crayfish are always friendly with each other.

6. _____ Shells help keep crayfish safe.

7. What do you think Uncle Bunny might do with Lefty's old suit?

   _____

Tony Takes a Dive

Read the story to find out how Uncle Bunny helped Tony Turtle.

1   Near the pond one day, I almost fell over an unusual rock. It was nearly round with a flat top. The bottom was green. I hadn't seen the rock before.

2   I leaned over to get a closer look. When I was just a whisker's length away, the rock talked. "Can you help me, Uncle Bunny?" it said.

3   "Bless my ears and whiskers!" I exclaimed. I jumped back a few steps. A head and four legs slowly poked out of the rock. I bent my head over so that I was looking upside down. Then I saw that the rock was Tony Turtle.

4   "I was eating berries from a bush up on the hill," Tony said. "When I reached for a berry, my foot slipped.

I rolled down the hill and landed on my back. Now I can't turn over."

5   I tried to push Tony, but he just turned in circles on his back. I pushed with my cane and with my paws. Nothing worked. Then I shut my eyes and pushed with all my might. Tony shot over the edge of the bank, still upside down. Then he dropped into the water, where he could turn right side up. "Thanks, Uncle Bunny!" he called. "I'm all right now!"

6   "I'm glad I could help, Tony," I answered. "All that pushing made me hungry. I think I'll go look for that berry bush."

152

Knowing the Words

Write the words from the story that have these meanings.

1. not like
most things _____
(Par. 1)

2. how long
something is _____
(Par. 2)

Working with Words

Circle the right word to finish the sentence. Then write the word in the blank.

1. I finished _____ grade.
(first   forest)

2. You are too _____ to
reach the top. (sharp   short)

The letter c can stand for the sound of s as in *city* and k as in *cat*. Circle words that have c as in *city*. Cross out words that have c as in *cat*.

(city)   ~~cat~~

3. crawl   cent   corner   fence

4. across   place   tractor   ice

5. once   color   dance   climb

6. clown   bounce   popcorn   face

7. magic   princess   picnic   can't

Reading and Thinking

1. Number the sentences to show what happened first, second, third, and last.

_____ Tony shot over the bank.

_____ Tony rolled down the hill.

_____ Tony was eating berries.

_____ Uncle Bunny pushed Tony.

2. Where did Uncle Bunny find

Tony? _____

3. Tony was on his back because

_____.

4. Tony looked like a rock because

_____.

5. Check the answer that shows Uncle Bunny got close to Tony.

_____ Uncle Bunny wanted a
closer look.

_____ Uncle Bunny was a
whisker's length away.

Fooling Mrs. Buzz

How would you act toward an angry bee? Read about Uncle Bunny and Mrs. Buzz.

1   Mrs. Buzz and I both like clover. Most times there is enough in the field for the two of us. But one day we were very grumpy about sharing.

2   I was finishing my breakfast when I found the freshest clover plant I had ever seen. I was ready to bite the fresh, pink blossom. Just then a loud, angry bee buzzed by my nose.

3   "I was here first! Leave that clover alone!" said Mrs. Buzz. She sat on the blossom that was almost in my mouth. My cheeks were so full of clover I could not answer.

4   "I'll teach you!" Mrs. Buzz cried. She flew from the blossom to my nose. Her stinger looked very sharp and long enough to reach my toes. I had to think fast!

5   "Sting my nose as much as you like, just don't sting my cane," I cried.

6   "Hum!" she buzzed. "You should not have told me that!" Then she landed on my cane. She poked her stinger down so hard the stinger bent right over. "Ouch!" Mrs. Buzz cried.

7   "Ouch, oh, ouch! My poor cane!" I cried, too, because I wanted Mrs. Buzz to think she had really hurt me. I limped away, rubbing my cane. From that day on I've always been nice to Mrs. Buzz. She may not be so easy to fool another time!

Knowing the Words

Write the words from the story that have these meanings.

1. unhappy _____
(Par. 1)

2. using together _____
(Par. 1)

3. flower _____
(Par. 2)

Working with Words

A word part that can be said by itself is called a **syllable.** Some words have two consonants between two vowels. These words can be divided between the consonants, as in *pic/nic.* Write each word below. Then draw a line to divide the word into syllables.

1. almost _____

2. blossom _____

3. rubbing _____

Circle the right word to finish each sentence. Then write the word in the blank.

4. Did you hear the _____ ?
(knew, knock, know)

5. I knew that was the _____
answer. (write, wrong, wrote)

Reading and Thinking

1. Number the sentences to show what happened first, second, third, and last.

_____ Uncle Bunny was eating.

_____ Uncle Bunny limped away.

_____ Mrs. Buzz poked her stinger down on the cane.

_____ Mrs. Buzz flew to Uncle Bunny's nose.

2. How did Uncle Bunny fool Mrs.

Buzz? _____

_____

3. Check two sentences that tell how Uncle Bunny and Mrs. Buzz were the same.

_____ They both got hurt.

_____ They both wanted clover.

_____ They were both grumpy.

The Gold Coat

Would Uncle Bunny like to have a gold coat? Why or why not?

1 Something bright and shiny caught my eye one morning as I walked by the pond. I looked closer. The shiny thing moved, but the water was very still.

2 I put my nose down to the water to get a better look. Suddenly I had a face full of water. The shiny thing splashed me! "Bless my ears and whiskers!" I exclaimed.

3 "Hello, Uncle Bunny," Gilda Goldfish said. "I didn't think you were so close to the water. I'm sorry I got you all wet!"

4 "Gilda, you look so shiny in the still water," I said. "I thought I had found some gold."

5 "Sometimes my bright, shiny coat is a problem," Gilda said. "If friends can see me, then enemies can see me, too. A green or brown coat might be better. I could hide just by being still on the bottom of the pond.'

6 "Lots of animals keep safe that way," I said. "Their coats are the color of their homes. Some animals even change color to match where they are."

7 "That sounds like a great idea," Gilda said. "When I need to hide, I must find some weeds or a rock."

8 "I'm glad my brown fur helps me hide," I said. "I wouldn't want to be Uncle Goldbunny!"

Reading and Thinking

1. Check the answer that tells what the story is mostly about.

    _____ Uncle Bunny's wet face

    _____ how animals keep safe

    _____ hiding in the weeds

Write the best word to finish each sentence.

2. Please _____ before you answer. (carry, hide, think)

3. We ran _____ the house in the rain. (toward, over, away)

Look at the picture on this page. Answer these questions about it.

4. Where is Gilda Goldfish hiding?

    _____

5. What is Sunny Sunfish wearing?

    _____

Working with Words

The ending **-y** added to a word can mean "full of." The word *rainy* means "full of rain." Write the meanings for these words. One is done for you.

dirty _*full of dirt*_

1. grassy _____

2. creamy _____

In rhyming words, only the beginning sound is different. In each sentence, write the word from the box that rhymes with the underlined word.

soap   bright   caught

3. Late at <u>night</u>, the stars are very

    _____.

4. I <u>hope</u> that I can find the

    _____.

5. My mother <u>bought</u> the fish that I

    _____.

Circle the right word to finish each sentence. Write the word in the blank.

6. We played, _____ we lost. (bit, bat, but)

7. Did you find your _____ ? (hit, hat, hot)

Flash Firefly

Read to find out why Flash Firefly didn't want to be called a fly.

1 "Grandpa, the stars are falling!" Sarah Jean called one night. I couldn't see anything in the sky. And I couldn't see Sarah Jean. Then I found her hiding under a bush. She was flat on the ground.

2 "Look out, here comes one now!" she shouted. As I turned around, Flash Firefly flew past me. He blinked his light and landed on a branch.

3 "Pick yourself up and come out, Sarah Jean," I chuckled. "There is nothing to be afraid of. It's Flash Firefly."

4 "Who is calling me a fly?" Flash asked. "I'm a beetle and proud of it."

5 "But you're called a firefly!" Sarah Jean called from under the bush.

6 "Names don't always mean just what they say. Sometimes I'm called a lightning bug, too, but I can't make lightning," Flash said. "I would like to stay, but my friend Blinky is calling." Flash blinked his light and flew away.

7 "I didn't hear anything, Grandpa," Sarah Jean said.

8 "That's because fireflies use their lights the way we use words," I said.

9 "I guess the stars were not falling at all," Sarah Jean laughed. "Flash and Blinky were just having a little talk!"

158

Reading and Thinking

1. Check the answer that tells what the story is mostly about.

   _____ stars falling from the sky

   _____ Uncle Bunny's walk

   _____ how Sarah Jean learns about fireflies

2. Why was Sarah Jean afraid? _____

   _____

3. How is a firefly like a fly? _____

   _____

Write **R** by the real things. Write **M** by the make-believe things.

4. _____ Stars fall to the ground.

5. _____ Fireflies make lightning.

6. _____ Fireflies are beetles.

Working with Words

Fill in each blank with the right pair of letters to make a word.

ar   er   or

1. Will you read me a st_____y?

2. We worked with flash c_____ds.

3. She took h_____ book home.

The letter g can stand for the sound of j as in cage and g as in girl. Circle words that have g as in cage. Cross out words that have g as in girl.

cage   girl

4. glass   large   hungry   goose

5. orange   gold   tag   together

Write the compound words from the story that have these meanings.

6. thing of
   any kind _____
   (Par. 1)

7. insect that
   makes light _____
   (Par. 2)

In each sentence, circle two words with the same vowel sound as the word in dark print.

8. **soap**   Wear your coat when you walk down the road.

9. **grow**   I can throw the ball low.

159

The Champion Jumper

Who is the champion jumper? Read to find out.

1   I used to think I was the best jumper in the meadow. Now I know that isn't true. Carol Anne and I were eating in the clover field one day. "Grandpa!" she said. "Someone has been eating our clover."

2   "Rabbits crabbits!" I shouted. "Just wait until I get my paws on the one who did this!"

3   "You'll never catch the champion jumper!" a voice called. I turned around. Just then Jumper, the grasshopper, sprang over my head.

4   "Champion jumper!" I cried. "We can have a contest. That will show who is the champion jumper! If you win, Jumper, I'll share this field with you. If I jump farther, you'll have to eat your lunch somewhere else." We both got ready.

5   I shook myself and took a deep breath. I was ready to take my best leap. Jumper shouted, "Go!" I took off and sailed far over the clover patch. I landed in the next meadow.

6   Jumper pushed herself into the air and opened her wings. She flew over my head and landed on the far side of the meadow.

7   "Well, I guess that shows I'm not the best jumper after all," I said. "We'll be sharing this field from now on. Why don't we begin by eating lunch together right now?"

Reading and Thinking

1. Uncle Bunny is Carol Anne's

_____.

2. Who jumped first in the contest?

_____

Write **T** if the sentence is true.
Write **F** if it is not true.

3. _____ Uncle Bunny didn't think he
could win the contest.

4. _____ Uncle Bunny learned
something about himself.

5. _____ Uncle Bunny keeps his
word.

6. What do you think Uncle Bunny
and Jumper did after lunch?

_____

_____

Working with Words

Circle words that have _c_ as in _city_.
Cross out words that have _c_ as in _cat_.

city   cat

1. picture   uncle   bounce   nice

2. popcorn   corner   face   cut

3. fence   across   candle   dance

An _'s_ at the end of a word may be
used to show that something belongs
to someone. Change these groups of
words using _'s_.

4. the clover of the rabbit

the _____ clover

5. the legs that belong to Jumper

_____ legs

6. the lunch of the grasshopper

the _____ lunch

Circle the right word to finish each
sentence. Then write the word in the
blank.

7. I can't _____ of it.
(think, thank, tent)

8. She _____ into the apple.
(bat, bit, but)

Pokey Snail

Did you ever trip over your own feet? Read this story about Pokey Snail.

1 One summer morning I was hopping down the path too fast. I stumbled and crashed to the ground! "Grandpa, are you hurt?" a little voice called. I picked myself up. I looked and saw Sonny stretched across the path. I had fallen over him.

2 "My bones are shaken and my fur is dirty," I replied, "but I'm all right. What are you doing?"

3 "I'm waiting for Pokey Snail to come home to his shell," Sonny said. He pointed to a shell by the path.

4 "Pokey takes his house with him," I said. "He's always at home anywhere. Pokey is inside, taking a nap." I tapped on the shell.

5 Little by little, a sleepy Pokey appeared. "I grew tired and stopped to rest. How did your fur get so dirty, Uncle Bunny?" Pokey asked.

6 "I tripped over Sonny," I said.

7 "I'm not surprised," Pokey laughed. "You rabbits have so many feet! I don't see how you can make them work together!"

8 "I have only four feet," Sonny said. "How many do you have, Pokey?"

9 "I have just one foot. It's my whole bottom side," Pokey said.

10 I started off down the path. When I looked back, I saw Sonny. He was down on his stomach, trying to move along on one "foot" just like Pokey.

Knowing the Words

Words that mean the same or nearly the same are **synonyms.** Circle two synonyms in each sentence below.

1. I laughed and Sonny chuckled.

2. My path is my road to the field.

Working with Words

Fill in each blank with the right pair of letters to make a word.

sh   ch

1. Foxes _____ased Uncle Bunny.

2. Sarah Jean hid under a bu_____.

Write these words. Draw a line to show the two syllables in each word.

3. ladder _____

4. corner _____

Add the word part **un-** to these words to finish the sentences below. One is done for you.

friendly   fair   lock   true

The game was *unfair*.

5. The new girl is _____.

6. Please _____ the door.

7. The last story is _____.

Reading and Thinking

1. Where did Sonny find Pokey's

    shell? _____

2. Number the sentences to show what happened first, second, third, and last.

    _____ Pokey appeared.

    _____ Sonny crawled like Pokey, on one foot.

    _____ Uncle Bunny stumbled.

    _____ Uncle Bunny tapped on Pokey's shell.

Write **T** if the sentence is true.
Write **F** if it is not true.

3. _____ Sonny was surprised that Pokey had just one foot.

4. _____ Sonny didn't know that Pokey was in his shell.

5. _____ Pokey is a speedy animal.

Sam Saves the Day

Read the story to find out how Uncle Bunny's cane helped the baby robins.

1 "Uncle Bunny! Hurry, please!" Sam Sparrow called to me. "We have to save Rosie's babies."

2 "Bless my ears and whiskers!" I cried. "What's wrong? Aren't the babies in the nest?"

3 "A storm cracked the branch where Rosie Robin has her nest. The branch is about to break," Sam shouted. "The babies are all alone in the nest. We have to help!"

4 We soon reached Rosie's tree. I could see that the branch was going to break very soon. Sam wasn't strong enough to lift the nest, and my paws were not made for climbing trees. We had to find another way.

5 "Maybe you can hop up on those rocks, Uncle Bunny," Sam said. "Then you can reach out and get the nest." I got myself up on the rocks, but I still couldn't reach the nest.

6 "Try your cane, Uncle Bunny," Sam said. My cane was just long enough. I pulled the nest toward me. At last I could lift it off the branch. Sam flew with me as I climbed off the rocks. Then the branch broke.

7 "My babies!" Rosie cried as she came back from finding food. "Where are my babies?"

8 "Sam's quick thinking kept your family safe," I explained.

9 "Thank you both!" Rosie said. "What good friends you are!"

Knowing the Words

Write the words from the story that have these meanings.

1. broke _____
   (Par. 3)

2. move up _____
   (Par. 6)

Working with Words

Circle the right word. Write it in the blank.

1. Hold on to the _____ of the kite. (string   spring)

2. We planted a _____ in the yard. (tree   free)

3. Say the word *bake.* Listen to the vowel sound of the word. In each word below, circle the two letters that stand for that sound.

   afraid   stay   away   paint

The letter *g* can stand for the sound of *j* as in *cage* and *g* as in *girl.* Circle words that have *g* as in *girl.* Cross out words that have *g* as in *cage.*

⬭girl   ~~cage~~

4. gift   village   wagon   bag

5. danger   grumpy   large   again

6. dog   strange   orange   game

Reading and Thinking

1. Why is the story called "Sam Saves the Day"? _____

   _____

   _____

Write **T** if the sentence is true.
Write **F** if it is not true.

2. ____ Uncle Bunny climbs trees.

3. ____ Sparrows aren't very strong.

4. What do you think Rosie Robin may do after feeding the babies?

   _____

   _____

Worms Don't Tell

Can you keep a secret? See if you can guess Sonny's secret.

1 Sonny is keeping some kind of secret. Tomorrow is my birthday. It could be a birthday secret!

2 This morning he was lying under a tree. He was holding his mouth shut with both front paws. "What is wrong with your mouth, Sonny?" I asked.

3 "I'm trying to keep a secret," he said. "I'm so excited. I have to tell someone soon."

4 "I'll keep the secret if you share it with me," I told him.

5 "Oh, I can't, Grandpa," Sonny said. "You are part of the secret!"

6 "Well, you can always trust an earthworm with a secret," I said.

7 "That is a wonderful idea!" Sonny cried. Sonny looked all over but couldn't find an earthworm. He looked by rocks and under trees and in the grass. He looked like he would pop!

8 Just then Rosie Robin flew by. "Can I help?" she asked Sonny. "I'm an expert at finding worms." Rosie pushed her bill deep into the ground. Soon she pulled out a worm.

9 "Thank you, Rosie," Sonny called. Then he sat down and whispered to the worm for a long time.

10 I was very curious. I suppose I'll know soon. Sonny said, "When the Forest Story Teller tells just one more story, all of us will know."

Knowing the Words

Write the words from the story that have these meanings.

1. someone good
at something _____
(Par. 8)

2. wanting
to know _____
(Par. 10)

Working with Words

Use these words to make compound words. Then use the compound words to finish each sentence below.

earth   birth   worm   day

1. Come to my _____ party.

2. A bird found an _____.

An 's at the end of a word may be used to show that something belongs to someone. Change these groups of words using 's.

3. the secret of Sonny

_____

4. the nest of the bird

_____

5. the branch of the tree

_____

Reading and Thinking

1. Check the answer that tells what the story is mostly about.

_____ keeping a secret

_____ a worm

_____ trouble with Sonny's mouth

2. What did Rosie Robin do to find an earthworm for Sonny?

_____

3. Check the sentence that tells why Sonny was holding his mouth.

_____ His tooth hurt.

_____ It was full of carrots.

_____ He was keeping a secret.

4. Why couldn't Sonny share his

secret with Uncle Bunny? _____

_____

5. Check the sentence that tells why the worm can keep the secret.

_____ Worms live in the ground.

_____ Worms have no legs.

_____ Worms cannot talk.

6. What do you think Sonny's secret

is? _____

A Well-Kept Secret

How do you know that Uncle Bunny has lots of friends in the forest?

1 "A rabbit's birthday should start with a carrot," I thought. I hopped toward the best carrot patch. I stopped when I saw something strange. Mrs. Buzz was showing Betsy Bear the tree where she keeps her honey. Most times they don't get along at all.

2 Farther along I stopped once more. I saw Red Squirrel. He was digging nuts for Barnie Raccoon.

3 At last I came to the carrot patch. Carol Anne and Sarah Jean had their cheeks stuffed with carrots. "These are for Sonny's secret. Don't chew them!" Carol Anne said.

4 By that time I was very hungry. I ate my fill of carrots. The sun was so warm I stretched out for a nap. Spotty Whitetail came to wake me. "Sonny needs you to come right now!" Spotty shouted.

5 When I reached the woods, I heard Sonny. "Over here, Grandpa," he called. I leaped over a bush and saw Sonny. He was carrying the biggest carrot cake I ever saw.

6 Voices from all over the forest cheered, "Happy birthday, Uncle Bunny!" One by one, my friends popped out of their hiding places.

7 "Bless my ears and whiskers!" I cried with surprise. "You are the best friends a rabbit could have!"

Reading and Thinking

1. Number the sentences to show what happened first, second, third, and last.

   ____ Uncle Bunny's friends cheered, "Happy birthday!"

   ____ Uncle Bunny saw some strange things happening.

   ____ Uncle Bunny took a nap.

   ____ Uncle Bunny decided to eat carrots for breakfast.

2. Write three things that were in Uncle Bunny's birthday cake.

   _____

Working with Words

Rewrite these words to mean more than one. Remember to change the *y* to *i* before adding **-es.**

1. country _____

2. city _____

3. family _____

4. Say the word *keep.* Listen to the vowel sound in the word. In each word below, circle the two letters that stand for that sound.

   feet   each   seed   deep

The spelling of some base words is changed before an ending is added. Words such as *happy* must have the *y* changed to *i* before adding an ending. Endings are word parts like **-er, -est,** and **-ed.** Change the *y* to *i* and add the endings to these words. One is done for you.

   carry + ed *carried*

5. heavy + est _____

6. hurry + ed _____

7. merry + er _____

8. hungry + est _____

Knowing the Words

Write the story words that have these meanings.

1. good or great

   <u>wonderful</u>
   _(Par. 2)

2. place to keep coats

   <u>closet</u>
   _(Par. 5)

3. went that way

   <u>headed</u>
   _(Par. 5)

Reading and Thinking

1. This story is mostly about

   ___ Marta's chair.

   ✓ Marta's surprise.

   ___ Marta's breakfast.

   Words such as *he, she,* and *it* take the place of other words. Read these sentences. Then fill in the blanks.

   Marta shouted as she ran.

   She stands for *Marta* .

2. Her mom laughed as she talked.

   She stands for <u>her mom</u> .

3. My dad talked as he worked.

   He stands for <u>my dad</u> .

3

Reading and Thinking

Put each word in the right blank.

   nose   hair   leash

1. She wiggled her _____ <u>nose</u>

2. My dog has a new _____ <u>leash</u> ___

3. Does Nicky have short _____ <u>hair</u> ?

Circle the right answer.

4. What will Marta do next?

   go to the library

   (take Nicky home)

   feed the birds

5. What helped Aunt Rosa train Nicky?

   <u>a book</u>

Working with Words

Circle the best word for each sentence. Then write it in the blank.

1. Nicky _____ <u>ran</u> _____ to Marta

   can   (ran)   pan

2. Marta walked her _____ <u>dog</u>

   (dog)   does   did

3. Nicky wiggled her _____ <u>ear</u>

   eat   each   (ear)

5

Knowing the Words

Write the story words that have these meanings.

1. walked fast

   <u>trotted</u>
   _(Par. 1)

2. rope used to hold an animal

   <u>leash</u>
   _(Par. 2)

3. ran after

   <u>chased</u>
   _(Par. 2)

Reading and Thinking

1. What is the name of Lee's dog?

   <u>Bigfoot</u>

   Why do you think he is named that?

   <u>He has big feet.</u>

   _____

2. What happened first in the story? Put **1** by it. What happened next? Put **2** by it. Put **3** by the thing that happened last.

   _3_ Marta called to Christy and Joe.

   _2_ Marta saw Lee and her dog.

   _1_ Marta took Nicky to the park.

7

Reading and Thinking

1. What will Nicky's collar have on it?

   <u>a round tag with Marta's</u>

   <u>name and phone number on it</u>

2. Why did Marta buy two dishes?

   <u>one for food and one for water</u>

   _____

3. Why did Marta pick a blue collar

   and blue dishes? <u>She likes blue</u>

   <u>best.</u>

Working with Words

Circle the best word for each sentence. Then write it in the blank.

1. The birds will _____ <u>fly</u> _____ away

   try   bright   (fly)

2. His hair is _____ <u>black</u>

   break   (black)   drink

3. I am _____ <u>glad</u> _____ you are here

   flew   (glad)   blue

4. Who will win the _____ <u>prize</u> ?

   (prize)   place   grass

9

Knowing the Words

Write the story words that have these meanings.

1. someone you like a lot

   <u>friend</u>
   (Par. 1)

2. someone who can carry things

   <u>carrier</u>
   (Par. 4)

Circle the three words in each line that belong together.

3. (house) book (park) (store)
4. (bark) fly (wiggle) (jump)
5. soup (lunch) (dinner) (breakfast)
6. ball (friend) (neighbor) (aunt)

Reading and Thinking

1. This story is mostly about
   ✓ Nicky and the mail.
   ___ a bone for Nicky.
   ___ Mom's surprise.

2. Why does Nicky bark so much?

   She thinks the mail carrier is

   not a friend.

3. Can you think of a way to make Nicky stop barking?

   (Answers will vary.)

11

Reading and Thinking

Some of these sentences are about **real** things, things that could happen. Write **R** by them. The other sentences are about things that could not happen, **make-believe** things. Write **M** by them.

1. _R_ A dog can run and play.
2. _M_ A house can talk.
3. _R_ A dog likes bones.
4. _M_ A dog likes to read.
5. Why does Mrs. Smith like her job? ___ She likes to walk

   and talk to everyone.

13

Learning to Study

Write each set of words in A-B-C order.

1. mail bark know

   <u>bark</u>

   <u>know</u>

   <u>mail</u>

2. work ears please

   <u>ears</u>

   <u>please</u>

   <u>work</u>

3. friend carrier drink

   <u>carrier</u>

   <u>drink</u>

   <u>friend</u>

Reading and Thinking

Put each word in the right blank.

   started petted burned

1. He <u>started</u> to go away.

2. The wood <u>burned</u> well.

3. We <u>petted</u> the cat.

Write **R** by the sentences that are about **real** things. Write **M** by the sentences about **make-believe** things.

4. _M_ Dogs can bake bread.
5. _R_ People can bake bread.
6. _R_ People bake bread in an oven.
7. _M_ An oven keeps food cool.

15

Working with Words

A **base** word is a word without an ending. The words in each row have the same **base** word. Circle the ending of each one. Then write the **base** word in the blank.

1. call(ing)   2. burn(ing)
   call(ed)   burn(ed)
   call(s)   burn(s)

   <u>call</u>   <u>burn</u>

Circle the best word for each sentence. Then write it in the blank.

3. We'll eat <u>when</u> he comes.
   then (when) check

4. Please finish <u>those</u> apples.
   chase (those) shoes

171

Reading and Thinking

1. Marta and Lee went to the creek because <u>it was cool</u>

   <u>there</u>.

2. Why couldn't Nicky find any fish after she jumped in? <u>They</u>

   <u>hid from her.</u>

3. Write **1, 2,** and **3** by these sentences to show what happened first, next, and last.

   _3_ Nicky jumped into the water.
   _1_ Lee said, "Stop for a while!"
   _2_ Nicky sniffed the water.

Learning to Study

Write each set of words in A-B-C order.

1. tired idea creek

   <u>creek</u>

   <u>idea</u>

   <u>tired</u>

2. quiet sniffed fish

   <u>fish</u>

   <u>quiet</u>

   <u>sniffed</u>

3. splash cool jumped

   <u>cool</u>

   <u>jumped</u>

   <u>splash</u>

17

Write the story words that have these meanings.

1. run after

_____chase_____
_(Par. 3)

2. moved the head up and down

_____nodded_____
_(Par. 6)

3. people who live near you

_____neighbors_____
_(Par. 7)

Put a check by the meaning that fits the underlined word in each sentence.

4. Is it <u>hard</u> to make new friends?
___ something not soft
_✓_ something not easy to do

5. I will <u>watch</u> Nicky play.
___ thing that tells time
_✓_ look at

1. What kind of dog is Flash?

_____collie_____

2. This story is mostly about
___ Marta playing with Nicky.
_✓_ a new neighbor.
___ Nicky's ball.

3. How will Nicky and Marta help Mike with his dog? _(Answers will vary.)_

4. Flash can't do any tricks

because __he is not trained__

19

1. This story is mostly about
___ Nicky playing.
_✓_ Nicky finding a kitten.
___ Nicky holding a kitten.

2. The four dogs were barking

because __a little cat was on__

__top of the car__

3. What makes you think that

Nicky likes kittens? _(Answers will vary.)_

Circle the best word for each sentence. Then write it in the blank.

1. This ___cat___ likes me.
(cat) call cut

2. I will ___get___ a drink.
gave got (get)

Write **-ing** or **-ed** in each blank.

3. I talk ___ed___ with her yesterday.

4. She want ___ed___ to work.

5. Now she is help ___ing___ us.

Circle the right word for each sentence. Then write it in the blank.

6. Mike is my best ___friend___
ground proud (friend)

7. I need a ___drink___ of water.
trick (drink) break

21

Look at each picture and circle the sentence that goes with it.

1. (Nicky is playing outside.)
Nicky is playing in the house.

2. Nicky sleeps on Marta's bed.

(Nicky sleeps in her basket.)

3. Who fixed dinner? ___Dad___

4. How did Nicky carry the kitten?

__in her mouth__

5. Why did Marta stay outside?

__(Answers will vary.)__

23

Circle the best word for each sentence. Then write it in the blank.

1. Nicky's collar has a ___tag___.
(tag) than tail

2. Nicky can be a ___quiet___ dog.
get (quiet) paint

3. The little kitten was ___wet___.
pet met (wet)

Write these sentences. Use one of the shorter words from the box to stand for the words that are underlined.

we'll	isn't	can't	didn't	I'm

4. <u>We will</u> be there.

__We'll be there.__

5. He <u>did not</u> go.

__He didn't go.__

6. The kitten <u>is not</u> hurt.

__The kitten isn't hurt.__

7. <u>I am</u> hungry.

__I'm hungry.__

8. Flash <u>cannot</u> do tricks.

__Flash can't do tricks.__

1. This story is mostly about
___ warming the milk.
___ talking about dogs.
_✓_ the kitten's new home.

Fill in the blanks.

2. Mom said, "Good idea," as she warmed the milk.

She stands for ___Mom___.

3. Mom found a box and lined it with a blanket.

_It_ stands for ___box___.

Circle the best word for each sentence. Then write it in the blank.

1. The milk is too ___hot___
hit (hot) hat

2. The kitten's eyes are ___big___
(big) bag buy

3. Marta's mom made a ___bed___
back (bed) bird

4. They have a ___new___ pet.
now not (new)

Read these words and look at the pictures.

Marta's mom   her mom's hand

You can see that you add _'s_ when you want to show that the hand belongs to Mom. Now write these names the same way.

5. Marta ___Marta's___ hand

6. Mike ___Mike's___ hand

25

172

Knowing the Words

Write the story words that have these meanings.

1. someone who keeps you well

   _____ doctor _____
   (Par. 3)

2. to be well

   _____ healthy _____
   (Par. 3)

3. to look over with care

   _____ check _____
   (Par. 4)

Circle the three words in each line that belong together.

4. (arms) flowers (feet) (hands)
5. (eyes) (ears) doctor (mouth)
6. hair (brown) (white) (black)

Reading and Thinking

1. This story is mostly about
   ____ pets who are not well.
   ____ a mean doctor.
   ✓ keeping pets healthy.

2. What four things did the doctor check on Nicky and Inky?

   _____ coats _____

   _____ eyes _____

   _____ ears _____

   _____ mouths _____

3. What do you think Marta can do to keep her pets healthy?

   (Answers will vary.)

   _____

   _____

27

Reading and Thinking

Put each word in the right blank.

   puppy   learn   door

1. Please open the _____ door _____.

2. Children _____ learn _____ at school.

3. My _____ puppy _____ has black eyes.

4. Write **1, 2,** and **3** by these sentences to show what happened first, next, and last.

   _3_ Marta was glad to see her friends.

   _2_ Nicky barked and ran to the door.

   _1_ There was a knock on the door.

29

Working with Words

Circle the best word for each sentence. Then write it in the blank.

1. Can you read this _____ book _____?
   cook   look   (book)

2. Marta _____ met _____ Allen today.
   mail   (met)   mean

3. Nicky pounded her _____ tail _____ on the floor.
   (tail)   fill   well

The missing word in each sentence sounds like *right*. Change the *r* in *right* to *f*, *l*, or *n*. Write the new words. The first one is done.

4. *fight* _____ light _____ night

Use the words you made in sentences.

5. Please turn off the _____ light _____.

6. We will not _____ fight _____ over the toys.

7. It rained last _____ night _____.

Knowing the Words

Write the story words that have these meanings.

1. not hard

   _____ easy _____
   (Par. 1)

2. what you call someone

   _____ name _____
   (Par. 1)

Circle the three words in each line that belong together.

3. (walk) look (trot) (run)
4. (head) (tail) trick (feet)
5. (good) mean (great) (wonderful)

Reading and Thinking

1. This story is mostly about
   ____ how to pet your dog.
   ✓ a meeting at Marta's.
   ____ Mike's dog.

2. What did Marta say a dog must know first?

   _____ its name _____

3. Tell one important lesson that Lee learned. _____ You have

   to show a dog you're happy

   it did something right.

4. Why do you think a dog learns faster if you say "good dog"?

   (Answers will vary.)

   _____

   _____

Reading and Thinking

1. This story is mostly about
   ✓ brushing dogs.
   ____ brushing Marta's hair.
   ____ Marta's dad.

2. Marta's dad said Nicky looked like a _____ string mop _____.

3. Why should you talk quietly and pet your dog when you brush it?

   (Answers will vary.)

   _____

   _____

   _____

Working with Words

Circle the best word for each sentence. Then write it in the blank.

1. Birds like to _____ use _____ hair in their nests.
   us   up   (use)

2. I can _____ bake _____ bread.
   back   (bake)   book

3. I _____ like _____ to brush my dog.
   little   (like)   let

Read these words and look at the pictures.

   cat   cats

You can see that you add *s* to show that you mean more than one cat. Write these words so that they mean more than one.

4. dog _____ dogs _____

5. bird _____ birds _____

6. ear _____ ears _____

33

Knowing the Words: Word meaning from context (1–2); Classification (3–5). **Reading and Thinking**: Main idea (1); Facts and details (2–3); Drawing conclusions (4).

31   173

Reading and Thinking

Put each word in the right blank.

special   bath   letter

1. Why is today so ___special___?

2. Nicky likes her ___bath___.

3. Marta wrote a ___letter___.

4. Who trained Nicky to sit?

   ___Aunt Rosa___

5. What is going to happen soon?

   ___a dog show___

6. This letter is mostly about
   ___ Marta and her friends.
   ___ the special trick.
   _✓_ Nicky.

Learning to Study

Write each set of words in A-B-C order.

1. trained   bath   special
   ___bath___
   ___special___
   ___trained___

2. care   splash   trick
   ___care___
   ___splash___
   ___trick___

3. pet   basket   sleeps
   ___basket___
   ___pet___
   ___sleeps___

Reading and Thinking

Put each word in the right blank.

hide   clean   delighted

1. My hands are ___clean___.

2. I am ___delighted___ to see you.

3. Will Nicky ___hide___ this bone from me?

4. Why do you think that Marta's grandmother and grandfather like dogs? _____

   (Answers will vary.)

Working with Words

Circle the best word for each sentence. Then write it in the blank.

1. Nicky has a cold ___nose___.
   (nose)   not   now

2. We will ___take___ a walk.
   talk   (take)   tail

The missing word in each sentence sounds like *make*. Change the *m* in *make* to *b*, *t*, or *w*. Write the new words.

3. ___bake___   ___take___   ___wake___

Use the words you made in sentences.

4. May we ___take___ a walk?

5. I like to ___bake___ bread.

6. Did Nicky ___wake___ you?

You know that *Mom's hand* means "the hand of Mom." Add *'s* when you write these names to show what belongs to each.

7. Dad   ___Dad's___ coat

8. Mike   ___Mike's___ book

9. Nicky   ___Nicky's___ teeth

Knowing the Words

Write the story words that have these meanings.

1. work you do

   ___job___
   (Par. 1)

2. made a low sound

   ___growled___
   (Par. 5)

Put a check by the meaning that fits the underlined word in each sentence.

3. The blanket will <u>brush</u> Nicky's nose.
   ___ thing used to fix hair
   _✓_ move over softly

4. Will Dad <u>play</u> with Nicky?
   _✓_ have fun
   ___ a show

Reading and Thinking

1. Who cleaned up after breakfast? ___Marta___

2. How did Inky help? ___He___ ___drank the milk.___

Write **R** by the sentences that are **real** things. Write **M** by the sentences that are about **make-believe** things.

3. _R_ People can make beds.

4. _M_ Dogs can make beds.

5. _M_ Cats can weed flowers.

6. _R_ People can weed flowers.

Reading and Thinking

Put each word in the right blank.

streams   hose   dry

1. We use a ___hose___ to water our flowers.

2. ___Streams___ of water ran down the window.

3. Is the paint ___dry___?

Write **R** by the sentences that are about **real** things. Write **M** by the sentences about **make-believe** things.

4. _M_ A yard can walk.

5. _R_ A dog can walk.

6. _R_ Birds can fly.

7. _M_ Dogs can fly.

Working with Words

Circle the best word for each sentence. Then write it in the blank.

1. She likes to ___pick___ flowers.
   pet   pan   (pick)

2. Sit ___back___ and read.
   (back)   bake   best

3. I like ___that___ book.
   think   thank   (that)

Fill in the missing vowel (*i*, *o*, or *u*) so the sentence makes sense.

4. Write on the l_i_ne.

5. Please give Nicky a b_o_ne.

6. May Nicky _u_se this pan?

Fill in each blank with **str** or **spr** so the sentence makes sense.

7. Here is a ball of ___str___ing.

8. I will ___spr___ay the grass.

9. Don't walk in the ___str___eet.

Put each word in the right blank.

cost   spend   bicycle

1. I have a new ___**bicycle**___.

2. I will ___**spend**___ my own money.

3. Does this ball ___**cost**___ much?

Fill in the blanks.

4. Flash's ball fell so Nicky carried it.

   It stands for ___**ball**___.

5. Marta and Nicky were happy because they were helping.

   They stands for ___**Marta**___ and ___**Nicky**___.

6. Nicky was carrying the ball as she ran.

   She stands for ___**Nicky**___.

Circle the best word for each sentence. Then write it in the blank.

1. Did Marta ___**train**___ Nicky?
   day   tail   (train)

2. Can you ___**hear**___ Nicky bark?
   heel   (hear)   head

3. Put on your warm ___**coat**___.
   (coat)   cook   clean

Change each underlined word to two words. Write them on the line.

4. Flash <u>didn't</u> have a ball.

   ___**did not**___

5. This <u>isn't</u> my bicycle.

   ___**is not**___

Circle the right letters for each sentence. Then write them in the blank.

6. I st___**ar**___ted to sit up.
   er   (ar)   ir

7. This book is too sh___**or**___t.
   (or)   er   at

8. Did the salesp___**er**___son help?
   or   (er)   ar

43

Write the story words that have these meanings.

1. moved on the air

   ___**floated**___
   (Par. 2)

2. trees with leaves that stay green

   ___**evergreens**___
   (Par. 2)

3. came to the ground

   ___**landed**___
   (Par. 2)

Put a check by the meaning that fits the underlined word in the sentence.

4. Did Marta know how to throw the airplane <u>right</u>?

   ___ not on the left

   _✓_ not the wrong way

Put each word in the right blank.

owned   proud   evergreens

1. I am ___**proud**___ of my dog.

2. We planted ___**evergreens**___ in our yard.

3. Mike ___**owned**___ a new toy.

4. Write **1**, **2**, and **3** by these sentences to show what happened first, next, and last.

   _2_ Nicky shook Mike's toy.

   _1_ Mike got an airplane.

   _3_ Marta said that she would buy another airplane.

5. Why does Marta want to buy Mike a new airplane?

   ___(Answers will vary.)___

45

---

1. When you are weeding, why do you have to know the flowers from the weeds?

   ___(Answers will vary.)___

2. Why did Nicky try to jump on the broom? ___**She wanted to play.**___

3. What did Marta do to make Nicky understand she was not playing a game? ___**She shouted and shook the broom.**___

Read each sentence and circle the word that is made of two shorter words. Write the two words on the lines.

1. You can sweep the (sidewalk).

   ___side___   ___walk___

2. Nicky did not (understand).

   ___under___   ___stand___

3. Will (someone) please help?

   ___some___   ___one___

Circle the best word for each sentence. Then write it in the blank.

4. Please ___**show**___ us a trick.
   who   (show)   those

5. Where are your ___**shoes**___?
   this   who's   (shoes)

6. Nicky will ___**chase**___ me.
   shook   (chase)   shout

Look at each picture and circle the sentence that goes with it.

1. (Nicky likes the water.)

   Nicky does not like the water.

2. A mother can work.

   (A mother can read.)

3. (He loves Bigfoot.)

   He doesn't like Bigfoot.

4. Where are the children working with Bigfoot?

   ___at Lee's house___

   How do you know? ___(Answers will vary.)___

Write these sentences. Use one shorter word for the two words that are underlined.

1. She <u>does not</u> know my name.

   ___She doesn't know my name.___

2. Bigfoot <u>will not</u> sit.

   ___Bigfoot won't sit.___

3. <u>It is</u> a beautiful day.

   ___It's a beautiful day.___

4. <u>I am</u> glad today.

   ___I'm glad today.___

Write these words so that they mean more than one. One is done for you.

   house   _houses_

5. mother   ___mothers___

6. dog   ___dogs___

7. boy   ___boys___

47   **49**

Knowing the Words

Write the story words that have these meanings.

1. thing that shows pictures

   <u>television</u>
   (Par. 1)

2. ideas or ways of doing

   something <u>plans</u>
   (Par. 1)

3. room used for cooking

   <u>kitchen</u>
   (Par. 1)

Put a check by the meaning that fits the underlined word in each sentence.

4. Nicky <u>can</u> shut the door.

   ____ a thing to hold food

   ✓ knows how to

5. I must <u>check</u> for the newspaper.

   ____ make a line

   ✓ look with care

51

Reading and Thinking

1. Why do you think Marta's dad didn't open the door himself?

   (Answers will vary.)

   _____

2. Do you think Nicky will shut the

   door again? _____

   Why or why not? _____

   (Answers will vary.)

   _____

3. Write **1, 2,** and **3** by these sentences to show what happened first, next, and last.

   2 Marta's dad looked for the newspaper.

   1 Marta's dad watched television.

   3 Marta saw Nicky's new trick.

Reading and Thinking

1. Why did Nicky wake up?

   Inky jumped on her.

   _____

Put each word in the right blank.

   wonderful   wake   piece

2. Warm bread smells

   <u>wonderful</u>.

3. Please give me a <u>piece</u> of bread.

4. Will you <u>wake</u> me?

Working with Words

The missing word in each sentence sounds like *stop*. Change the *st* in *stop* to *t, m,* or *p*. Write the new words and put them in the right sentences.

1. <u>top</u>   <u>mop</u>   <u>pop</u>

2. Some popcorn didn't <u>pop</u>.

3. I hit the <u>top</u> of my head.

4. Clean the floor with a <u>mop</u>.

Circle the right letters for each sentence. Then write them in the blank.

5. They walked in the p<u>ar</u>k.

   er   ir   (ar)

6. What happened f<u>ir</u>st?

   ar   or   (ir)

Add *'s* to these words to show what belongs to each one.

7. dog   the <u>dog's</u> collar

8. cat   the <u>cat's</u> head

9. bird   the <u>bird's</u> nest

10. kitten the <u>kitten's</u> ball

53

Knowing the Words

Write the story words that have these meanings.

1. near

   <u>close</u>
   (Par. 4)

2. so glad

   <u>delighted</u>
   (Par. 5)

Circle the three words in each line that belong together.

3. (paws) (tail) soft (head)

4. (glad) (delighted) (pleased) sad

5. paint (grass) (park) (yard)

55

Reading and Thinking

1. This story is mostly about

   ____ a fast car.

   ____ Mike's bicycle.

   ✓ Marta helping Flash.

2. Why was Flash walking in the

   street by himself? Mike wasn't

   there to tell him "no."

3. How had the dog lessons

   helped Flash? He came when

   Marta called him.

4. Write **1, 2,** and **3** to show what happened first, next, and last.

   3 Flash ran to Marta.

   2 Marta called to Flash.

   1 Marta played in her yard.

Reading and Thinking

1. What did Marta think was

   better than a bath? using the

   hose to get clean

2. Why did Marta's dad help her

   call Mike? Marta was

   too muddy to go inside.

Put each word in the right blank.

   belongs   mud   swimsuit

3. Flash has <u>mud</u> on him.

4. This book <u>belongs</u> to Allen.

5. My <u>swimsuit</u> is too big.

Working with Words

Fill in the missing vowel (a, i, or o) so each sentence makes sense.

1. You did a f<u>i</u>ne job.

2. Wash off with the h<u>o</u>se.

3. We will m<u>a</u>ke the bed.

Use the underlined words to make a new word to finish each sentence.

4. A <u>suit</u> that you wear when you

   <u>swim</u> is called a <u>swimsuit</u>.

5. A <u>yard</u> that is in <u>back</u> of a

   house is called a <u>backyard</u>.

Circle the best word for each sentence. Then write it in the blank.

6. Do not <u>shout</u> at me.

   show (shout) chair

7. Our house is <u>clean</u>.

   boat (clean) stay

57

Reading and Thinking

Put each word in the right blank.

quiet   lapping   television

1. The cat is ___lapping___ up the milk.

2. What ___television___ show do you like best?

3. We were ___quiet___ in the library.

4. This story is mostly about
   - _✓_ Inky's trick.
   - ___ Mom and Dad needing quiet.
   - ___ Nicky wants to play.

Working with Words

To make a word mean more than one, add -es if the word ends in s, ss, ch, sh, or x. Write these words so that they mean more than one.

1. lunch   ___lunches___

2. dish   ___dishes___

3. box   ___boxes___

Fill in the missing letter so the sentence makes sense.

4. I like to h_e_lp my dad.

5. Nicky j_u_mped into the water.

6. Marta p_i_cked up the ball.

Fill in the missing letters so each sentence makes sense.

ar   or   ur

7. Did Nicky h_ur_t her paw?

8. Can we play in your y_ar_d?

59

Knowing the Words

Write the story words that have these meanings.

1. part of a house ___basement___
   (Par. 1)

2. close ___near___
   (Par. 1)

3. to wash off ___clean___
   (Par. 5)

4. top part of a house ___upstairs___
   (Par. 5)

5. place in back of a house ___backyard___
   (Par. 6)

Circle the three words in each line that belong together.

6. (upstairs) idea (house) (kitchen)
7. (chair) (table) mail (picture)
8. box (brush) (broom) (mop)
9. (ran) sat (raced) (chased)

Reading and Thinking

1. If you paint in dusty air, how will the paint look? ___dusty___

   (Answers will vary.)

2. How did Marta's mom and dad's work look when it was done?

   ___good___

Look at each picture and circle the sentence that goes with it.

3. (Dad paints with a brush.)

   Dad is brushing Nicky.

4. (Joe helps at home.)

   Joe is not helping.

61

Reading and Thinking

1. Where did Mom and Dad go after dinner? ___the backyard___

2. Marta wanted to do the dishes because ___she wanted everyone to help___

3. Write 1, 2, and 3 to show what happened first, next, and last.
   - _2_ Marta washed the dinner dishes.
   - _3_ Marta washed the pets' dishes.
   - _1_ Marta had dinner.

Working with Words

In each row, circle the two letters in each word that make the same sound you hear in the underlined word.

toy   p(oi)nt   b(oy)   n(oi)se

1. show   kn(ow) (ow)n thr(ow)
2. see   tr(ee) f(ee)t pl(ea)se
3. found   d(ow)n ar(ou)nd br(ow)n
4. mean   n(ee)d n(ea)r r(ea)d

Circle the best word for each sentence. Then write it in the blank.

5. Do you like this ___game___?
   same   (game)   name

6. Mike found ___his___ money.
   hit   him   (his)

7. This is my ___best___ hat.
   (best)   nest   last

8. Marta hit the ___ball___.
   (ball)   call   tell

Circle each c that stands for the sound of s in these words.

9. on(c)e   12. pie(c)e
10. doctor   13. be(c)ause
11. fen(c)e   14. come

63

Knowing the Words

Write the story words that have these meanings.

1. push on

   ___lean___
   (Par. 3)

2. what a dog has around its neck ___collar___
   (Par. 7)

3. made a noise in the nose ___snorted___
   (Par. 7)

Circle the three words in each line that belong together.

4. mail (library) (store) (park)
5. (heel) (sit) (stay) found
6. (collar) (leash) (tag) bird
7. (move) (walk) (run) stay

Reading and Thinking

Look at each picture and circle the sentence that goes with it.

1. Dogs and cats do not like each other.

   (The dog and cat are friends.)

2. (Marta likes to read books.)

   Marta never reads books.

3. Why did Bigfoot snort?

   ___He didn't like it when he fell over.___

4. Why do you think Mr. Barker knows a lot about dogs?

   ___(Answers will vary.)___

   _____

65

Reading and Thinking

1. This story is mostly about
   ___ the prize ribbons.
   ___ going to the library.
   _✓_ the dog show.

2. What five things do the children need for their dog show?

   _____ signs _____

   _____ rope _____

   _____ number signs _____

   _____ ribbons _____

   _____ prizes _____

3. Who will make the copies?

   _____ Lee _____

Working with Words

Circle the right letters for each sentence. Then write them in the blank.

1. Do you w__or__k hard?
   ar ⊚or⊚ ir

2. It is your t__ur__n to play.
   ar or ⊚ur⊚

3. The dog sn__or__ts loudly.
   er ⊚or⊚ ar

Circle the best word for each sentence. Then write it in the blank.

4. Can you make your __bed__?
   bag ⊚bed⊚ big

5. Mike wrote a __letter__.
   listen last ⊚letter⊚

6. We filled the __pan__ with milk.
   ⊚pan⊚ pet pop

Use the underlined words to make a new word to finish each sentence.

7. <u>Corn</u> that can <u>pop</u> when you cook it is __popcorn__.

8. A <u>walk</u> that is by the <u>side</u> of the street is a __sidewalk__.

67

Reading and Thinking

1. Why did Marta ask if Dad had to go away the day of the show?

   __She thought he might not be__

   __able to come to the show.__

   _____

Fill in the blanks.

2. Mom and Dad talked as they painted.
   They stands for

   __Mom and Dad__

3. Marta's dad answered, and he said, "No, Marta."

   He stands for __Marta's dad__

Working with Words

The missing word in each sentence sounds like *new*. Change the *n* in *new* to *bl*, *fl*, and *thr*. Write the new words, and put them in the right sentences.

1. __blew__ __flew__ __threw__

2. The wind __blew__ hard.

3. I __threw__ my dog a ball.

4. The bird __flew__ away.

Circle the best word for each sentence. Then write it in the blank.

5. Marta will __brush__ Nicky.
   grass ⊚brush⊚ growl

6. Will Dad __try__ to be here?
   dry play ⊚try⊚

The ending **-er** means "more" and the ending **-est** means "most." Add the endings **-er** and **-est** to these base words.

	-er	-est
clean	*cleaner*	*cleanest*
7. kind	__kinder__	__kindest__
8. fast	__faster__	__fastest__

69

Knowing the Words

Write the story words that have these meanings.

1. to lean over

   __bend__
   (Par. 1)

2. moved hand up and down

   __waved__
   (Par. 2)

3. thinking of others

   __kind__
   (Par. 4)

Put a check by the meaning that fits the underlined word in each sentence.

4. <u>Why</u> did Mom say that?
   _✓_ a word that asks something
   ___ a word of surprise

5. <u>Why</u>, Marta, that's beautiful!
   ___ a word that asks something
   _✓_ a word of surprise

Reading and Thinking

Put each word in the right blank.
   waved   bend   tired

1. Those jobs make me __tired__.

2. I __waved__ to my friend.

3. The flowers will __bend__ in the wind.

4. How are Marta and Mrs. Peters helping each other?

   __Marta is holding the basket,__

   __and Mrs. Peters will make__

   __the ribbons. (Answers may__

   __vary.)__

71   178

Reading and Thinking

Look at each picture and circle the sentence that goes with it.

1. Nicky is asleep in her basket.
   ⊚Nicky has a bone.⊚

2. Inky is jumping.
   ⊚Inky is drinking milk.⊚

3. ⊚Mike cuts the grass.⊚
   Mike weeds the flowers.

Put each word in the right blank.
   spray   shiny   enter

4. Marta has __shiny__ new shoes.

5. We __spray__ the flowers.

6. Please knock and __enter__.

Working with Words

Write these words so that they mean more than one.

1. sign __signs__

2. idea __ideas__

3. can __cans__

Circle the best word for each sentence. Then write it in the blank.

4. Dad __cooked__ breakfast.
   cooking ⊚cooked⊚

5. Mom is __working__ outside.
   works ⊚working⊚

6. Grandfather __wants__ to help.
   ⊚wants⊚ wanting

7. We can plant a __garden__.
   good ⊚garden⊚ judge

8. Do you live in the __city__?
   coat ⊚city⊚ cut

9. Please __let__ me go.
   ⊚let⊚ lot last

10. She has a funny __hat__.
    ⊚hat⊚ hit hot

73

1. Why would the pet shop be a good place for a dog show sign?

   People who have or like

   dogs come to that shop.

   _____

2. To tell where the prizes came from at the show, Mike will say, "Today's prizes are from

   Mr. Barker's pet store

   _____ ''.

3. Do you think Mr. Barker will be a good judge for the show? ___

   Why do you think so? _____

   (Answers will vary.)

Circle the best word for each sentence. Then write it in the blank.

1. What is ___better___ than a bath?
   basket   basement   (better)

2. Please ___check___ your work.
   (check)   collar   closet

Write these sentences. Use one shorter word for the two words that are underlined.

3. I do not have a sign.

   I don't have a sign.

4. That is great!

   That's great!

5. We will be glad.

   We'll be glad.

6. That is not a good place.

   That isn't a good place.

Put each word in the right blank.
   entered   glitter   prizes

1. This ___glitter___ will make the ribbon shiny.

2. Lee ___entered___ her dog in the show.

3. We will give ribbons for

   ___prizes___ .

4. How did Mike and Marta get a can full of money? ___People___

   gave it to them to enter

   the dog show.

Sometimes the letter c stands for the sound s makes as in city. Circle each c that stands for the sound of s in these words.

1. (c)ircle   3. (c)ity
2. cat   4. car

Circle the best word for each sentence. Then write it in the blank.

5. I know ___what___ you want.
   (what)   shut   that

6. I'll be ___there___ in a minute.
   chair   (there)   where

7. The ___wind___ blew hard.
   will   well   (wind)

8. Please ___fill___ my dish.
   fall   fell   (fill)

Put each word in the right blank.
   permission   paste   nodded

1. Marta ___nodded___ her head.

2. I have ___permission___ to go.

3. ___Paste___ will make the ribbon stick together.

4. Who called the people who run the park? ___Mom___

5. How do you think Mike and Joe felt while they were helping with the ribbons? ___(Answers will vary.)___

Write each set of words in A-B-C order.

1. people   money   other

   ___money___

   ___other___

   ___people___

2. busy   paste   cost

   ___busy___

   ___cost___

   ___paste___

3. glitter   ribbon   city

   ___city___

   ___glitter___

   ___ribbon___

1. Who made the number signs?

   ___Marta and Mike___

2. What do you think Nicky was sniffing on Grandmother's coat?

   ___Aunt Rosa (Answers may vary.)___

3. Write 1, 2, and 3 to show what happened first, next, and last.

   _3_ Aunt Rosa said, "Nicky, sit!"

   _2_ Grandfather talked to Marta.

   _1_ Mom knocked on Marta's door.

In each sentence, circle the word that is made of two shorter words. Write the two words on the lines.

(Everyone) met at Lee's house.

Every   _one_

1. Do you ever play (football)?

   foot   _ball_

2. (Grandmother) gave Marta a hug.

   Grand   _mother_

Circle the best word for each sentence. Then write it in the blank.

3. They played with ___their___ toys.
   chair   (their)   where

4. I am ___third___ in line.
   while   short   (third)

In each row, circle the two letters in each word that stand for the vowel sound you hear in the underlined word.

5. day   p(ai)nt   tr(ai)n   st(ay)
6. each   gr(ee)n   m(ea)n   f(ee)t
7. know   c(oa)t   sh(ow)   (ow)n
8. proud   d(ow)n   ab(ou)t   n(ow)

Write the story words that have these meanings.

1. afraid

   <u>nervous</u>
   (Par. 1)

2. a number of people together

   <u>crowd</u>
   (Par. 1)

3. place for a dog show

   <u>ring</u>
   (Par. 5)

Put a check by the meaning that fits the underlined word in each sentence.

4. Marta <u>saw</u> Lee standing there.

   ___ something that cuts wood

   _✓_ used her eyes

5. Marta walked into the <u>ring</u>.

   ___ sound a telephone makes

   _✓_ a circle where a show is

Put each word in the right blank.

   crowd   judge   nervous

1. The <u>crowd</u> of people clapped.

2. Who will <u>judge</u> the dog show?

3. She is <u>nervous</u> about the show.

4. How did Nicky feel at the dog show? <u>(Answers will vary.)</u>

5. How do you think Nicky and Marta will do in the show?

   <u>(Answers will vary.)</u>

83

1. Why couldn't Mr. Barker pick a winner? <u>All of the dogs</u>
   <u>in the ring were well trained.</u>

2. What makes you think that Marta did not know about the gold ribbon?

   <u>She looked in surprise at</u>
   <u>Mrs. Peters.</u>

3. Why did the crowd pick Nicky to win? <u>(Answers will vary.)</u>

Circle the best word for each sentence. Then write it in the blank.

1. I am still <u>clapping</u> for Nicky.

   clapped   (clapping)

2. Nicky <u>jumped</u> over Marta.

   (jumped)   jumping

Add 's to these words to show what belongs to each one. Write the new word.

3. judge   <u>judge's</u>   smile

4. Marta   <u>Marta's</u>   turn

5. Nicky   <u>Nicky's</u>   ribbon

Circle g when it stands for the sound of g in go.

6. (g)ood   8. judge

7. (g)arden   9. a(g)ain

85

Write the words from the story that have these meanings.

1. face hairs <u>whiskers</u>
   (Par. 1)

2. did over and over <u>practiced</u>
   (Par. 3)

3. did write <u>wrote</u>
   (Par. 7)

Circle the right word to finish the sentence. Then write the word in the blank.

1. The team ran a good <u>race</u>.
   (face, case (race))

2. Hit the ball with the <u>bat</u>.
   (bell (bat) bed)

1. Check the answer that tells what the story is mostly about.

   ___ how children learn

   ___ Uncle Bunny's big ears

   _✓_ how Uncle Bunny learned to write

2. Look at the picture. Check the two sentences that tell about the picture.

   _✓_ Uncle Bunny wears glasses.

   ___ Uncle Bunny drives a car.

   _✓_ Uncle Bunny can write.

3. Uncle Bunny found a box under a

   <u>window at the school</u>

Some things are real and some are make-believe. Write **R** by real things. Write **M** by make-believe things.

4. _M_ Rabbits can write.

5. _R_ Children can learn.

6. _M_ Squirrels can talk.

87   **180**

Write the words from the story that have these meanings.

1. kind of plant <u>clover</u>
   (Par. 1)

2. storm sound <u>thunder</u>
   (Par. 1)

3. loud sounds <u>noise</u>
   (Par. 3)

The words *come* and *go* have meanings so different that they are **opposite.** Make a line from each word in the first list to the word in the second list with the opposite meaning.

4. wet ———— noise

5. quiet ⤫ dry

6. stay ———— leave

A word without any endings is a **base word.** The base word of *talking* is *talk*. Circle each base word below.

1. (listen)s   2. (push)ed   3. (eat)ing

Sometimes one word stands for two words. The word *didn't* stands for *did not*. Write a word from the story that can stand for each pair of words.

4. we will <u>we'll</u>
   (Par. 4)

5. I am <u>I'm</u>
   (Par. 5)

1. Check the answer that tells what the story is mostly about.

   ___ Uncle Bunny having lunch

   _✓_ where animals go during a storm

   ___ black clouds

2. Where were Mrs. Whitetail and Spotty when they heard thunder?

   <u>under the trees</u>

3. Check the sentence that tells why the deer moved to the open field.

   ___ They went there to eat.

   ___ Spotty tried to run away.

   _✓_ A storm was coming.

4. Why do you think Spotty tried to run away? _____

   <u>(Answers will vary.)</u>

Knowing the Words

Write the words from the story that have these meanings.

1. a small place __patch__
   (Par. 1)

2. hair cut from sheep __wool__
   (Par. 4)

3. between cold and warm __cool__
   (Par. 7)

Circle the three words in each row that belong together.

4. (morning) year (night) (afternoon)
5. (coats) (hats) feet (shoes)
6. wet (cold) (warm) (hot)
7. (happy) (sad) (angry) old

Learning to Study

Number the words to show A-B-C order for each list.

1. __3__ lamb   2. __2__ cool
   __1__ carrot   __1__ answered
   __2__ friend   __3__ patch
   __4__ wool   __4__ wrote

Reading and Thinking

1. Check the answer that tells what the story is mostly about.
   ____ keeping people warm
   ____ being cool in the summer
   __✓__ Sniffles giving his wool

2. What was Sniffles doing by the pond? __looking at himself__
   __in the water__

3. Sniffles thought he looked funny because __he didn't have__
   __his coat anymore__

Words such as *he, his, she,* and *her* take the place of other words. Read these sentences. Fill in the blanks.

4. Sniffles cried as he saw himself.
   He stands for __Sniffles__.

5. Uncle Bunny ate his carrots.
   His stands for __Uncle Bunny__.

Write **R** by the real things. Write **M** by the make-believe things.

6. __M__ Lambs wear gloves.
7. __R__ Coats are made from wool.

91

Knowing the Words

Write the words from the story that have these meanings.

1. one who takes something __thief__
   (Par. 1)

2. nut from oak tree __acorn__
   (Par. 3)

Check the meaning that fits the underlined word in each sentence.

3. We clean up leaves in the <u>fall.</u>
   __✓__ part of year before winter
   ____ to drop suddenly

4. I <u>wave</u> as I leave for school.
   __✓__ make a good-bye sign
   ____ rolling water

Working with Words

Write **S** beside each word that stands for one of something. Write **P** by each word that stands for more than one.

1. __S__ noise   2. __P__ acorns

Circle the right word to finish each sentence. Then write the word in the blank.

3. The cold wind __blew__ in our faces. (threw, flew, (blew))

4. The cars hit with a loud __crash__. (splash, (crash), flash)

Reading and Thinking

1. Red Squirrel planted an acorn in what part of the year? __fall__

Write **T** if the sentence is true.
Write **F** if it is not true.

2. __T__ Oak trees grow from acorns.

3. __T__ The story happens in winter.

4. Red could not find his acorn because __he didn't remember__
   __where he put it__

5. What do you think Red did after he ran up the tree? _____
   __(Answers will vary.)__

6. How did Red Squirrel feel when he thought someone took his nut?
   __angry__

93

Knowing the Words

Write the words from the story that have these meanings.

. black and white animal __skunk__
   (Par. 1)

. small animals such as bees and ants __insects__
   (Par. 3)

Words that mean the same or nearly the same are called **synonyms.** Circle two synonyms in each row.

. (begin) stop call (start)
. bird (rabbit) skunk (bunny)
. listen catch (see) (look)
. (run) car (hurry) dog

Learning to Study

Number the words to show A-B-C order for each list.

. __4__ turn   2. __1__ carrot
  __2__ patch   __2__ growl
  __1__ bee   __3__ happen
  __3__ skunk   __4__ safe

95

Reading and Thinking

1. Check the answer that tells what the story is mostly about.
   ____ how rabbits hide under berry bushes
   ____ a frightened dog
   __✓__ how skunks keep safe

2. Number the sentences to show what happened first, second, third, and last.
   __3__ The skunks danced.
   __2__ Uncle Bunny heard a growl.
   __4__ The dog ran away.
   __1__ Uncle Bunny met the skunks.

Write the best word to finish each sentence below.

3. We heard the band and wanted to __dance__. (read, dance, believe)

4. The dog __growled__ at the loud noise. (growled, worked, laughed)

181

Knowing the Words

Write the words from the story that have these meanings.

1. a place to walk __path__
   (Par. 1)

2. insect bite __sting__
   (Par. 4)

In each row, circle the two words with opposite meanings.

3. (inside) little claws (outside)
4. long (push) hungry (pull)

Working with Words

An *'s* at the end of a word may be used to show that something belongs to someone. Add *'s* to each name. Write each name in the right blank.

Uncle Bunny__'s__   Betsy Bear__'s__

1. __Betsy Bear's__ burning nose

2. __Uncle Bunny's__ whiskers

Circle the right word to finish each sentence. Then write the word in the blank.

3. Please __bring__ your book with you. ((bring), string, spring)

4. The clothes are __clean__. ((clean), cream, string)

Reading and Thinking

1. Where did Betsy's path go?
   __to the stream__

2. What did Betsy find inside the tree? __honey__

3. The bees were angry because __Betsy took their honey__

Write **T** if the sentence is true.
Write **F** if it is not true.

4. __T__ Bears and bees eat honey.

5. __F__ Bears and bees make honey.

6. __F__ Bees are larger than bears.

7. What do you think Betsy did when she came out of the stream?
   __(Answers will vary.)__

97

Knowing the Words

Write the words from the story that have these meanings.

1. grassy field _____meadow_____
(Par. 1)

2. very close to _____against_____
(Par. 2)

Check the meaning that fits the underlined word in each sentence.

3. The kite <u>sailed</u> above the trees.
____ moved on water
_✓_ flew high

4. Joe is putting a <u>patch</u> on his coat.
____ place where carrots grow
_✓_ small piece of cloth

Working with Words

Write a word from the story that stands for each pair of words.

1. was not _____wasn't_____
(Par. 2)

2. could not _____couldn't_____
(Par. 5)

Reading and Thinking

1. Check two sentences that tell how Uncle Bunny and the foxes were the same.
_✓_ They were all clever.
____ They were all afraid.
_✓_ They were all good runners.

2. What did Uncle Bunny throw away before he ran? __his cane__

3. Where was Tricky chasing Uncle Bunny? __to Slick's hiding place__
_____(Answers may vary.)_____

4. When Uncle Bunny saw Tricky behind him, he may have felt
_____frightened_____

Write the best word to finish each sentence below.

5. The fox _____jumped_____ over the fence. (sang, jumped, sat)

6. The wind blew the _____leaves_____ off the trees. (mountain, leaves, sun)

7. The runner was so __fast__ she seemed to fly. (slow, new, fast)

99

Knowing the Words

Write the words from the story that have these meanings.

1. sends out light _____shines_____
(Par. 1)

2. between _____through_____
(Par. 1)

3. moving up and down ___bouncing___
(Par. 3)

4. small animal that builds webs _____spider_____
(Par. 3)

5. homes for spiders _____webs_____
(Par. 6)

Circle the three words in each row that belong together.

6. (spider) frog (ant) (bee)

7. airplane (sun) (moon) (star)

8. (tell) (say) carry (talk)

9. small (long) (high) tall

Working with Words

Walk and *talk* are **rhyming words.** In rhyming words, only the beginning sound is different. Change the *f* in *fine* to *l, m,* or *n* to make rhyming words. Write each new word.
(Words may be in any order.)

1. _____line_____

2. _____mine_____

3. _____nine_____

Reading and Thinking

Words such as *he, she,* and *it* take the place of other words. Read these sentences. Then fill in the blanks.

1. Willy sang as he worked. *He* stands for _____Willy_____

2. Willy's house moved as it caught the wind. *It* stands for _____
_____Willy's house_____

Write the best word to finish each sentence below.

3. I _____ran_____ to be at school on time. (ran, thought, ate)

4. The children moved the ___toys___ to the backyard. (street, toys, stairs)

5. The _____clock_____ showed w____ were late. (flag, chicken, clock)

6. Check the sentence that tells wh____ Uncle Bunny would have trouble in Willy Webb's house.
_✓_ Rabbits can't walk on strings.
____ The roof is too low.
____ There is only one bedroom

1__

Knowing the Words

Write the words from the story that have these meanings.

1. lights in the sky _____stars_____
(Par. 1)

2. closed and opened quickly _____blinked_____
(Par. 1)

Write **S** for each pair of words that have the same or nearly the same meanings (synonyms). Write **O** for each pair with opposite meanings.

3. little _S_ small

4. easy _O_ hard

5. wash _S_ clean

Circle the three words in each row that belong together.

6. (raccoon) carrot (rabbit) fish

7. water (paws) (eyes) (head)

8. (branch) (tree) star (leaves)

Reading and Thinking

1. Number the sentences to show what happened first, second, third, and last.
_3_ Barnie caught a fish.
_2_ Uncle Bunny followed Barnie.
_1_ Two "stars" blinked.
_4_ Uncle Bunny lost his fish.

2. How were Barnie's eyes like stars? __They were shining and__
__over Uncle Bunny's head.__

3. Check the answer that tells how Barnie and Uncle Bunny are different.
____ They both like to eat breakfast.
_✓_ Barnie likes fish, but Uncle Bunny likes carrots.

Write the best word to finish each sentence below.

4. The boat was _____sailing_____ on the lake. (wiggling, sailing, swimming)

5. I _____walked_____ quietly past the room. (walked, rolled, blinked)

103

Knowing the Words

Check the meaning that fits the underlined word in each sentence.

1. <u>Roll</u> the mud into a ball.
_✓_ make round
____ a kind of bread

2. The bears like to <u>play</u> outside.
____ a show to watch
_✓_ do a game or have fun

Use lines to match the words with opposite meanings.

3. laughing — coming

4. going — behind

5. ahead — crying

Working with Words

Write a word from the story that can stand for each pair of words.

1. it is _____it's_____
(Par. 2)

2. we are _____we're_____
(Par. 6)

3. that is _____that's_____
(Par. 6)

Make each word mean more than one by adding **-s.** Write the word.

4. forest _____forests_____

5. flower _____flowers_____

Reading and Thinking

Write **R** by the real things. Write **M** by the make-believe things.

1. _M_ Bears laugh at rabbits.

2. _M_ Bears talk to rabbits.

3. _R_ Bears scare rabbits.

Write the best word to finish each sentence below.

4. The loud horn will _____scare_____ the five boys. (learn, scare, feed)

5. I'll _____wash_____ my face and brush my hair. (light, move, wash)

6. José _____watched_____ the man play the game. (watched, told, knew)

7. We planted _____flowers_____ in the garden. (words, ideas, flowers)

1__

Knowing the Words

Words that mean the same or nearly the same are called **synonyms**. Use lines to match synonyms.

1. little — quick
2. close — tiny
3. fast — near

Working with Words

A **compound word** is made by putting two words together. Write a compound word for the underlined words below. One is done for you.

A word meaning <u>some</u> kind of <u>thing</u> is *something*.

1. A time <u>after</u> the <u>noon</u> time is

    _____afternoon_____.

2. A <u>bird</u> whose wings make a <u>humming</u> sound is a

    _____hummingbird_____

Fill in each blank with the right pair of letters to make a word.

ch   sh   th   wh

3. **wh** iskers
4. **th** is
5. **wh** eel
6. **th** ink
7. **ch** ange
8. **sh** ort

Reading and Thinking

1. How is a hummingbird different from most birds? <u>It is smaller and can "park" in the air.</u>

Write **R** by the real things. Write **M** by the make-believe things.

2. **M** Hummingbirds wear glasses.
3. **R** Hummingbirds eat insects.
4. **R** Hummingbirds are different from most birds.
5. **M** Hummingbirds wear shoes.
6. Check the answer that tells what a hummingbird nest may look like.
    - ✓ very small
    - ___ a box for shoes
    - ___ very large

107

Knowing the Words

Write the words from the story that have these meanings.

1. scared _____frightened_____ (Par. 1)
2. closed _____shut_____ (Par. 3)
3. cried out _____exclaimed_____ (Par. 7)

Circle the three words in each row that belong together.

4. (wings) (head) sky (beak)
5. (meadow) (field) lake (land)
6. fit (scared) (frightened) (afraid)

Working with Words

A **compound word** is made by putting two words together. Use these words to make two compound words.

fast   light   flash   break

1. _____flashlight_____
2. _____breakfast_____

Reading and Thinking

1. Check the answer that tells what the story is mostly about.
    - ✓ how Diver scared Uncle Bunny
    - ___ how hawks fly
    - ___ animals eating lunch

2. Write two things Diver Hawk did to frighten Uncle Bunny. _____He pointed his head down._____

    He began to drop.

3. Write **T** if the sentence is true. Write **F** if it is not true.
    - **F** The story takes place at night.
    - **F** Hawks cannot see very well.
    - **T** Hawks can fly very well.

Write the best word to finish each sentence below.

4. The house was _____quiet_____ after the party ended. (quiet, scared, angry)
5. My sister and her _____friends_____ took a trip. (field, friends, fence)

109

Knowing the Words

Write the words from the story that have these meanings.

1. how big or little something is _____size_____ (Par. 1)
2. one more _____another_____ (Par. 3)
3. very good, fine _____sharp_____ (Par. 4)
4. place where two sides come together _____corner_____ (Par. 6)

In each row, circle the two words with opposite meanings.

5. (down) off around (up)
6. tell (gone) say (came)
7. show (large) (small) bless

Working with Words

Circle the right word to finish each sentence. Then write the word in the blank.

1. My mother opened a _____can_____ of soup for lunch. ((can) cane)
2. Will you _____hide_____ the gift for the party? (hid (hide))
3. Does your new hat _____fit_____? ((fit) fight)

Reading and Thinking

1. Check the answer that tells what the story is mostly about.
    - ___ Uncle Bunny's supper
    - ✓ how an owl uses its ears
    - ___ night sounds in the forest

Write **T** if the sentence is true. Write **F** if it is not true.

2. **F** Uncle Bunny couldn't see Cynthia's ears because she didn't have any.
3. **T** Owls hear sounds from all around because they turn their heads almost around.
4. Check the sentence that tells how owls and rabbits are like each other.
    - ✓ They both have ears.
    - ___ They both eat carrots.
    - ___ They both can fly.

Write **R** by the real things. Write **M** by the make-believe things.

5. **R** Owls can hear very well.
6. **M** Owls can hear clover grow.
7. **R** Owl ears can't be seen.
8. **R** Owls hear better than rabbits.

111

Knowing the Words

Write the words from the story that have these meanings.

1. all of something _____whole_____ (Par. 3)
2. having great meaning _____important_____ (Par. 8)
3. laughed quietly _____chuckled_____ (Par. 9)

In each row, circle the two words with opposite meanings.

4. start (right) (wrong) begin
5. (new) forest trees (old)
6. sound noise (louder) (quieter)
7. (there) (here) now time

Learning to Study

Write each group of words in A-B-C order. Each group of words will make a sentence. Use a period or a question mark to end each sentence.

1. move didn't wagon Barnie the

    _____Barnie didn't move the wagon._____

2. whistles new Children silver like

    _____Children like new silver whistles._____

Reading and Thinking

1. Check the answer that tells what the story is mostly about.
    - ___ Biff's soft red feathers
    - ✓ friends arguing about things that are not really important
    - ___ how Uncle Bunny gets a new red coat

Words such as *he, she,* and *it* take the place of other words. Read these sentences. Then fill in the blanks.

2. Biff smiled as he talked.

    He stands for _____Biff_____.

3. Mrs. Coats sang as she worked.

    She stands for _____Mrs. Coats_____.

4. My coat is red, but it is shiny.

    It stands for _____my coat_____.

113

Knowing the Words

Check the meaning that fits the underlined word in each sentence.

1. Uncle Bunny likes to take a <u>rest</u> in the afternoon.
   - ____ that which is left
   - _✓_ time without work

2. The sun went down and I was <u>still</u> asleep.
   - ____ quiet
   - _✓_ up to this time

Working with Words

A word part that can be said by itself is called a **syllable.** Some words have two consonants between two vowels. These words can be divided between the consonants, as in *pic/nic*. In each word below, draw a line to divide the word into syllables.

1. c o t/t o n
2. a l/w a y s
3. w i n/d o w
4. a l/m o s t
5. m o n/k e y
6. s i l/l y
7. c h i m/n e y
8. e n/g i n e

115

Reading and Thinking

1. Check the answer that tells what the story is mostly about.
   - ____ how Uncle Bunny hurt his ear
   - _✓_ how Uncle Bunny slept through supper
   - ____ Gordy's loud, clear singing voice

2. Check the two words that tell about Gordy.
   - _✓_ friendly   ____ mean
   - ____ tired   _✓_ helping

Write the best word to finish each sentence below.

3. The ___fence___ needs to be painted again. (cotton, fence, word)

4. The new road is ___wide___ and even. (wide, green, late)

5. The ___nap___ made us feel much better. (dirt, engine, nap)

Knowing the Words

Write the words from the story that have these meanings.

1. touched lightly ___brushed___ (Par. 2)

2. makes angry ___bothers___ (Par. 3)

Check the meaning that fits the underlined word in each sentence.

3. Something with wings and tiny teeth flew <u>past</u> my face.
   - _✓_ by
   - ____ some time before

4. Uncle Bunny lost his <u>cane</u>.
   - ____ plant for making sugar
   - _✓_ stick for walking

Working with Words

Write a word from the story that can stand for each pair of words.

1. I will ___I'll___ (Par. 3)

2. you will ___you'll___ (Par. 5)

An *'s* shows that a thing belongs to someone. Change these words to show what belongs to someone.

3. bat ___bat's___ wings

4. Barnie ___Barnie's___ tail

Reading and Thinking

1. What animals were in the story?
   ___Uncle Bunny, Brown Bat,___
   ___and an insect___

2. What did the insect bite?
   ___Uncle Bunny's ears___

3. Brown Bat didn't want any carrots because ___she eats only___
   ___insects___

Write **T** if the sentence is true.
Write **F** if it is not true.

4. _T_ Uncle Bunny thinks bats are animals that help.

5. _F_ Brown Bat eats apples.

6. _F_ Uncle Bunny likes all insects.

11

Knowing the Words

Write the words from the story that have these meanings.

1. an open path under the ground ___tunnel___ (Par. 1)

2. something only a few know ___secret___ (Par. 1)

3. Check the meaning that fits the underlined word in the sentence.
   I sneezed so <u>hard</u> I fell over.
   - ____ not easy to do
   - _✓_ not soft

Learning to Study

To put words in A-B-C order you must first look at the first letter of each word. If the first letters are the same, look at the second letters. Number each list to show A-B-C order.

1. _4_ nose
   _1_ eyes
   _3_ mouth
   _2_ face
2. _3_ sound
   _2_ sneezed
   _4_ stream
   _1_ scratch

Reading and Thinking

1. Check the answer that tells what the story is mostly about.
   - ____ finding the secret tunnel
   - ____ Uncle Bunny's dirty face
   - _✓_ Whistler digging a tunnel

2. Number the sentences to show what happened first, second, third, and last.
   - _1_ Uncle Bunny heard digging and scratching.
   - _3_ Uncle Bunny got his face full of dirt.
   - _2_ Uncle Bunny sat down to wait for Whistler.
   - _4_ Uncle Bunny fell over onto his back.

Write **T** if the sentence is true.
Write **F** if it is not true.

3. _T_ A woodchuck's home is dark.

4. _T_ A woodchuck needs strong paws.

5. What do you think Uncle Bunny will do the next time he sees Whistler digging a tunnel?
   ___(Answers will vary.)___

119

Knowing the Words

Write the words from the story that have these meanings.

1. reached across ___stretched___ (Par. 4)

2. small insects ___ants___ (Par. 6)

Words that mean the same or nearly the same are called **synonyms.** Circle two synonyms in each row.

3. body (tiny) (small) seed
4. toward (sound) away (noise)
5. (begin) read answers (start)

Working with Words

Write the best word to finish each sentence below.

1. I ___wrote___ the answer. (wrote, rope, rode)

2. You took the ___wrong___ street. (rock, rest, wrong)

When **un-** is added to a word, it changes the meaning of the word. The word part **un-** means "not." *Unreal* means "not real." Add **un-** to these words to finish the sentences.

3. She was _un_hurt in the fall.

4. The food was _un_touched.

Reading and Thinking

1. Check the answer that tells what the story is mostly about.
   - _✓_ Uncle Bunny learning about how ants work
   - ____ seeds that walk and talk at the same time
   - ____ how Cookie Ant became so strong

2. How big was the seed that Cookie was carrying? ___ten times___
   ___bigger than Cookie___

3. How was Cookie helping the ant town? ___by taking a seed___
   ___to the town___

Write the best word to finish each sentence below.

4. The train went through the ___tunnel___ under the river. (mud, tunnel, water)

5. I ___brushed___ my hair before I left for school. (brushed, learned, practiced)

6. Take the dishes ___into___ the kitchen. (under, above, into)

121

Knowing the Words

Write the words from the story that have these meanings.

1. sides of the face under the eyes _____cheeks_____ (Par. 4)
2. wanting food _____hungry_____ (Par. 7)

Circle the three words in each row that belong together.

3. (nap) (dream) sight (sleep)
4. fly (chipmunk) (mouse) (squirrel)
5. (ran) (hurried) (scampered) sat

Working with Words

Write the best word to finish each sentence below.

1. Do you _____know_____ the new teacher? (know, nose, noise)
2. Did someone _____knock_____ on the door? (nest, lock, knock)

Write these compound words beside their meanings.

underground   sunset   afternoon

3. when sun goes down _____sunset_____
4. later than noon _____afternoon_____
5. under the ground _____underground_____

Reading and Thinking

1. What color were Chomper's stripes? _____black and white_____

2. Check two sentences that show Chomper was smaller than Uncle Bunny.

   ✓ Chomper ran between Uncle Bunny's legs.

   ✓ The ear of corn was bigger than Chomper.

   ___ Chomper's cheeks got very fat.

3. How are crows like chipmunks?
   _____They both eat corn._____

Write **R** by the real things. Write **M** by the make-believe things.

4. __M__ Lightning had lunch with Uncle Bunny.
5. __R__ Chipmunks put away food for the winter.
6. __R__ Chipmunks can carry lots of food in their cheeks.

123

Knowing the Words

Write the words from the story that have these meanings.

1. things to learn _____lessons_____ (Par. 2)
2. play make-believe _____pretend_____ (Par. 4)
3. made a short, quick move or sound _____popped_____ (Par. 9)

Circle the three words in each row that belong together.

4. (watch) (look) hide (see)
5. (hawk) deer (bobwhite) (crow)

Working with Words

In each sentence, circle three words with the same vowel sound as the word in dark print.

1. **now**   The (cow) (found) the sweet grass and gave a (loud) MOO!
2. **now**   (How) can I drive (around) the (mountain)?

Reading and Thinking

1. Check the answer that tells what the story is mostly about.
   ___ a circle of sleeping birds
   ✓ hiding lessons for the bobwhite babies
   ___ counting bobwhite babies

2. How many babies do Mr. and Mrs. Bobwhite have? _____16_____

3. What did the bobwhite babies pretend? _____that a hawk_____ _____was near_____

Write **T** if the sentence is true. Write **F** if it is not true.

4. __F__ Bobwhites sleep in trees.
5. __F__ Uncle Bunny's coat talks.
6. __T__ Bobwhites are afraid of hawks.

7. Check two words that tell about Peter Bobwhite.
   ___ large
   ✓ fuzzy
   ✓ clever

125

Knowing the Words

In each row, circle two words that have opposite meanings.

. see (close) (far) look
. (never) few (always) some
. cry break (sleep) (wake)

Working with Words

A word part that can be said by itself is called a **syllable.** Some words have two consonants between two vowels. These words can be divided between the consonants, as in pic/nic. In each word below, draw a line to divide the word into syllables.

. h a p/p y   3. w o n/d e r
. w h i s/p e r   4. t r a c/t o r

Walk and talk are **rhyming words.** In rhyming words, only the beginning sound is different. Write words that rhyme with spring by changing spr in spring to r or w.

. _____ring_____   6. _____wing_____

Then use each new word in the right sentence.

. The bird hurt its _____wing_____
. Will the school bell _____ring_____ ?

Reading and Thinking

1. Check the answer that tells what the story is mostly about.
   ___ Uncle Bunny's glasses
   ___ sleeping with noise
   ✓ finding a friend

Write the best word to finish each sentence below.

2. If you _____break_____ the toy, you must fix it. (jump, break, cry)
3. The _____noise_____ of the train kept us awake. (noise, rain, floating)
4. Move _____closer_____ to the front so you can see better. (later, closer, wider)

Read these sentences. Then fill in the blanks.

5. Bumbles sneezed as he cried.
   He stands for _____Bumbles_____.
6. Prickles saw me as she walked by.
   She stands for _____Prickles_____.
7. The cane slipped as it hit the ice.
   It stands for _____cane_____.

127

Knowing the Words

Words that mean the same or nearly the same are called **synonyms.** Circle two synonyms in each row.

1. dirty (rock) (stone) clean
2. (road) (path) knees toes
3. straight curves (looked) (saw)

Working with Words

Words that end in s, ss, x, sh, or ch add **-es** to show more than one. Rewrite these words to show more than one. One is done for you.

dress _____*dresses*_____

1. box _____boxes_____
2. pass _____passes_____
3. flash _____flashes_____

Circle the right word to finish each sentence. Then write the word in the blank.

4. We _____rode_____ bikes through the forest. (rod (rode))
5. The car slipped on the _____ice_____. (is (ice))
6. Most mornings I _____hop_____ to the carrot patch. ((hop) hope)

Reading and Thinking

1. Number the sentences to show what happened first, second, third, and last.

   _2_ Uncle Bunny and Chubby pushed and pulled a stone.
   _3_ The stone rolled away into the grass.
   _4_ Chubby thanked Uncle Bunny for his help.
   _1_ Uncle Bunny fell down.

2. Because a stone was in the way, the mice couldn't _____make their_____ _____road straight_____

Write **T** if the sentence is true. Write **F** if it is not true.

3. __T__ Chubby can run faster on straight roads.
4. __F__ The road was already straight.
5. __T__ The stone was heavy.
6. The next time Uncle Bunny hops through the meadow, he may _____(Answers will vary.)_____

129

185

Page 131

Knowing the Words

Check the meaning that fits the underlined word in each sentence.

1. Did she <u>run</u> in the race?
- ✓ move fast on legs
- ___ what a machine does

2. The tree needs a <u>deep</u> hole.
- ___ having a low voice
- ✓ a long way to the bottom

3. The children <u>watch</u> the puppy.
- ___ small clock
- ✓ look at

Learning to Study

To put words in A-B-C order you must first look at the first letter of each word. If the first letters are the same, look at the second letters. Number each list to show A-B-C order.

1.
- 4 stood
- 3 sleepy
- 2 secret
- 1 safe

2.
- 2 deep
- 3 island
- 1 bless
- 4 set

3.
- 4 muskrat
- 3 minute
- 1 acorn
- 2 maybe

4.
- 4 wonder
- 1 leap
- 2 weeds
- 3 wheel

Reading and Thinking

Use the groups of words in the box to finish the sentences below.

- it looked like a pile of weeds
- he could fix it
- he wanted to see what was there

1. Uncle Bunny jumped on the island because **he wanted to see what was there** .

2. Uncle Bunny thought Musky's house was an island because **it looked like a pile of weeds** .

3. Musky wasn't angry about his roof because **he could fix it** .

131

Page 13(3)

Knowing the Words

Write the words from the story that have these meanings.

1. a present **gift** (Par. 3)

2. with nothing wrong **perfect** (Par. 8)

Working with Words

Circle the right word to finish each sentence. Then write the word in the blank.

1. The snow is always **cold** .
(**cold** fold)

2. He got a new milk **cup** .
(cut **cup**)

When a word ends in *e*, the *e* may be dropped before adding **-ed** or **-ing**. Add **-ing** to these words. Then use the new words in the sentences below. One is done for you.

bounce + ing *bouncing*

3. leave + ing **leaving**

4. He is **leaving** the cane beside the tree.

5. I am **bouncing** a ball up and down.

Reading and Thinking

1. Check the answer that tells what the story is mostly about.
- ✓ finding the right gift
- ___ standing on hills or rocks
- ___ Uncle Bunny's nap

Write the best word to finish each sentence.

2. The right gift will make someone very **happy** .
(happy, lost, flat)

3. Please **cut** the grass.
(read, open, cut)

4. Check the group of words that tells about Glenda.
- ___ a very good singer
- ✓ thinking of others
- ___ not a good friend

13(3)

Page 135

Knowing the Words

Write the words from the story that have these meanings.

1. move the feet in water **paddle** (Par. 1)

2. evenly **smoothly** (Par. 1)

3. did swim **swam** (Par. 2)

In each row, circle the two words with opposite meanings.

4. (close) tiny (far) little

5. soap (last) (first) mud

6. smooth (loudest) (softest) gone

Working with Words

The ending **-er** means "more," so *prouder* means "more proud." The ending **-est** means "most," so *proudest* means "most proud." Add the endings **-er** and **-est** to these base words. One is done for you.

Joe is the tall *est* of six boys.

1. Donna is old **er** than Molly.

2. I was the loud **est** of the four.

Reading and Thinking

1. Write two things ducks must do to swim well.

paddle smoothly and wiggle their tails

Write **T** if the sentence is true. Write **F** if it is not true.

2. **T** Molly was a playful duck.

3. **T** Uncle Bunny wanted to help.

4. **T** Donna Duck taught her children not to be silly.

5. **F** Ducks are always afraid of rabbits.

6. **F** Baby ducks always know how to swim.

7. Molly was scared because **Uncle Bunny hid and shouted at her** .

Write the best word to finish each sentence.

8. Judy **hid** the keys in the basket.
(splashed, hid, woke)

9. The girl **waved** her hand to show she was ready.
(washed, bit, waved)

135 **186**

Page 13(7)

Knowing the Words

Write the words from the story that have these meanings.

1. surprised **startled** (Par. 1)

2. part of a tree **log** (Par. 3)

3. part of the mouth **tongue** (Par. 4)

Check the meaning that fits the underlined word in each sentence.

4. Does a <u>fly</u> have wings?
- ✓ insect
- ___ move in the air

5. I'm glad the show is <u>over.</u>
- ___ on the other side
- ✓ done, finished

6. My <u>ears</u> hurt from the noise.
- ___ parts of corn plants
- ✓ things used for hearing

Learning to Study

Number the words to show A-B-C order for each list.

1.
- 3 shy
- 1 here
- 4 startled
- 2 loud

2.
- 4 log
- 2 lady
- 1 glad
- 3 like

Reading and Thinking

1. Number the sentences to show what happened first, second, third, and last.
- 3 Uncle Bunny visited Mr. Bullfrog.
- 2 Uncle Bunny heard a noise.
- 4 Mr. Bullfrog told why he sings at night.
- 1 Uncle Bunny was asleep.

2. Check two answers that tell how Mr. Bullfrog's tongue is like yours.
- ✓ He uses it to eat.
- ___ He catches flies with it.
- ✓ He uses it to talk.

Write **R** by the real things. Write **M** by the make-believe things.

3. **R** Frogs can make noises.

4. **M** Rabbits can jump out of their fur.

Write the best word to finish each sentence below.

5. A frog's **tongue** is very long. (tongue, dress, car)

6. Uncle Bunny likes to **sleep** at night. (sleep, bark, fly)

13(7)

Knowing the Words

Words that mean the same or nearly the same are called **synonyms.** In each row below, circle the two words that are synonyms.

1. (closer) in out (nearer)
2. fly (see) (look) sky

In each row, circle the two words with opposite meanings.

3. came (slowly) (quickly) saw
4. always sometimes (many) (few)
5. (yes) (no) things always

Working with Words

Write the best word to finish each sentence below.

1. Angel likes to _____fly_____.
   (fly, try, cry)

2. _____Spring_____ is the best part of the year. (Spring, Thing, String)

Fill in each blank with the right pair of letters to make a word.

        ar or ur

3. The little bunny grew l_ar_ge.

4. I ate this m_or_ning.

5. We t_ur_ned the page to read.

Reading and Thinking

1. Put a check by two words that tell about Angel Butterfly.

   _✓_ happy   ____ crawling

   ____ angry   _✓_ flying

2. Look at the picture. Check the two sentences that tell about it.

   _✓_ Uncle Bunny is eating the carrot.

   ____ Uncle Bunny ate the carrot.

   _✓_ Angel is flying.

Write the best word to finish each sentence.

3. The small plant ___grew___ larger. (moved, came, grew)

4. My coat keeps me ___warm___. (little, warm, friendly)

139

Knowing the Words

Write the words from the story that have these meanings.

1. wall to hold back water ___dam___
   (Par. 1)

2. something done wrong ___mistake___
   (Par. 7)

Working with Words

Write the best word to finish each sentence below.

1. Storms can bring ___rain___. (rain, ran, run)

2. Can you ___say___ the new word? (said, sad, say)

3. I ___know___ the answer. (now, know, not)

An 's at the end of a word shows that a thing belongs to someone or something. Change these groups of words by using 's.

4. the branch of the tree

   the ___tree's___ branch

5. the home of Bonnie

   ___Bonnie's___ home

Reading and Thinking

1. What did Bonnie Beaver build in the stream near her home?

   ___a dam___

2. Check the answer that tells what the story is mostly about.

   ____ how beavers chew on fence posts

   _✓_ beavers cutting down trees

   ____ how to build a dam

3. Check two sentences that tell how Bonnie could use the tree she cut.

   _✓_ She could use the branches to fix her house.

   ____ She could use the tree for fence posts.

   _✓_ She could use the tree to make the dam stronger.

4. Check two words about Nibbler.

   _✓_ sorry   ____ angry

   _✓_ mixed-up   ____ excited

141

Reading and Thinking

. Check the answer that tells what the story is mostly about.

   ____ how swans swim

   _✓_ how Uncle Bunny goes across the pond

   ____ eating carrots for breakfast

ead these sentences. Then fill in the anks.

Sandy wiggled as she cleaned her feathers.

She stands for ___Sandy___.

The clover leaned as it grew.

It stands for ___the clover___.

Sal swam as she washed.

She stands for ___Sal___.

Working with Words

Write the best word to finish each sentence below.

1. I have a ___pin___ on my dress. (pen, pine, pin)

2. Can you ___ride___ the horse? (ride, red, roll)

3. That book is ___mine___. (win, mine, men)

4. Will you feed the ___cat___? (can, car, cat)

5. The boys ___cook___ their lunch. (cook, look, book)

When **re-** is added to a word, it changes the meaning of the word. The word part **re-** means "again." *Refill* means "fill again." Add **re-** to these words to finish the sentences.

6. I will _re_build the house.

7. Who will _re_do these papers?

8. Please _re_fill the tall jar.

9. Did you _re_write the test?

10. Did the station _re_run the show?

11. Please _re_tell the story.

143

Working with Words

Write a compound word for the underlined words in each sentence.

1. A <u>storm</u> that brings <u>snow</u> is a

   ___snowstorm___

2. A game with a <u>ball</u> and <u>basket</u> is

   ___basketball___

Write the best word to finish each sentence below.

3. Be sure to look over ___each___ answer. (each ears)

4. Uncle Bunny hid under a _bush_. (burn bush)

5. I'll soon be in ___third___ grade. (word third)

6. ___Try___ to do your best. (Try Fry)

Reading and Thinking

1. Number the sentences to show what happened first, second, third, and last.

   _2_ Uncle Bunny's glasses fell.

   _3_ Sunny found the glasses.

   _4_ Sunny pushed the glasses.

   _1_ Uncle Bunny hopped to the pool.

Write the best word to finish each sentence.

2. The child took the ___little___ puppy for a walk. (deep, little, clover)

3. Can you see your ___face___ in the glass? (family, idea, face)

Look at the picture with the story. Write the best word to finish each sentence about the picture.

4. There is a ___log___ in the pool. (school, log, cage)

5. ___Plants___ are growing at the bottom of the pool. (Flowers, Rabbits, Plants)

6. The water is ___clean___. (dirty, clean, moving)

145

In each row, circle the two words with opposite meanings.

1. (same) cold cool (different)
2. lake (long) (short) pond

Walk and *talk* are **rhyming words.** In rhyming words, only the beginning sound is different. The missing words below rhyme with *shook*. Change *sh* in *shook* to *l, b, c,* and *t.* Then write each new word in the right sentence.

1. __look__   3. __cook__

2. __book__   4. __took__

5. We __took__ the wrong road.

6. Did you read the __book__?

7. I can __cook__ dinner.

8. Did the car __look__ new?

Write the best word to finish each sentence below.

9. I have not __seen__ her before. (send seen)

10. We rode the __bus__ to school. (bone bus)

1. Check the answer that tells what the story is mostly about.

____ where Uncle Bunny is having dinner

_√_ meeting a new bird

____ Greta's safe trip

Read these sentences. Then fill in the blanks.

2. The stream sparkled as it splashed.

It stands for __stream__.

3. Sal swam as she talked to Uncle Bunny. *She* stands for __Sal__.

Write the best word to finish each sentence below.

4. The friends __write__ letters at camp. (tell, write, do)

5. Some animals __eat__ berries. (make, buy, eat)

6. Did you __drink__ the milk? (stay, drink, grow)

7. What may Greta do after Uncle Bunny leaves? _____
____(Answers will vary.)____

147

Circle the three words in each row that belong together.

1. (water) (stream) rock (pond)
2. drive (slip) (slide) (fall)
3. (rocks) (mud) (stones) stuck
4. (he) (she) (it) rabbit

Write the best word to finish each sentence below.

1. The class will __care__ for the bird. (care car)

2. Did someone __burn__ dinner? (barn burn)

Most words add **-s** or **-es** to show more than one. Words that end in *y* are different. In most words that end in *y*, change the *y* to *i*, and add **-es.** Change the words below to mean more than one. One is done for you.

berry *berries*

3. story __stories__

4. penny __pennies__

5. puppy __puppies__

6. library __libraries__

1. Check the answer that tells what the story is mostly about.

____ how Susie moved a rock from the bank

____ Uncle Bunny's wet whiskers

_√_ Susie Otter's new mud slide

2. How long did Susie work to make her slide? __a week__

3. Susie said she was sorry to Uncle Bunny because __she got him all wet__

4. Why doesn't Uncle Bunny like to get wet? __He gets cold when he is wet.__

5. Check three sentences that tell how Susie Otter is a hard worker.

_√_ Susie moved one big rock from the bank.

_√_ Susie moved plants and branches.

____ Susie went down the slide.

____ Susie shook water all over.

_√_ Susie moved lots of stones to make her new slide.

14

Circle two synonyms in each row.

1. (glad) claw stone (happy)
2. lost knew (rock) (stone)

The spelling of some base words is changed before an ending is added. Words such as *bat* must have the last letter doubled before adding **-ed** or **-ing.** Double the last letter and add the endings to these words to finish the sentences. One is done for you.

cut hit pet

(ed) The dog likes to be *petted*

1. (ing) We are __hitting__ the ball.

2. (ing) He is __cutting__ the cake.

Circle the right word to finish the sentence. Then write the word in the blank.

3. Did you read the __sign__? (nine (sign) fine)

4. I heard what he __said__ (said) (red, bed)

5. Please get the key to the __car__ (cap (car) can)

1. Check the answer that tells what the story is mostly about.

____ Lefty's missing claw

_√_ a crayfish's shell

____ a rock in the stream

2. What did Lefty's shell look like? __thin and shaped like Lefty__

3. Uncle Bunny knew Lefty was under the rock because __his claw was sticking out__

4. Why is Lefty called Lefty? __He lost his right claw in a fight. (Answers may vary.)__

Write **T** if the sentence is true. Write **F** if it is not true.

5. _F_ Crayfish are always friendly with each other.

6. _T_ Shells help keep crayfish safe.

7. What do you think Uncle Bunny might do with Lefty's old suit? __(Answers will vary.)__

151

Write the words from the story that have these meanings.

1. not like most things __unusual__ (Par. 1)

2. how long something is __length__ (Par. 2)

Circle the right word to finish the sentence. Then write the word in the blank.

1. I finished __first__ grade. (first) forest)

2. You are too __short__ to reach the top. (sharp (short))

The letter *c* can stand for the sound of *s* as in *city* and *k* as in *cat*. Circle words that have *c* as in *city*. Cross out words that have *c* as in *cat*.

(city) ~~cat~~

3. ~~crawl~~ (cent) ~~corner~~ (fence)
4. ~~across~~ (place) ~~tractor~~ (ice)
5. (once) ~~color~~ (dance) ~~climb~~
6. ~~clown~~ (bounce) ~~popcorn~~ (face)
7. ~~magic~~ (princess) ~~picnic~~ ~~can't~~

1. Number the sentences to show what happened first, second, third, and last.

_4_ Tony shot over the bank.

_2_ Tony rolled down the hill.

_1_ Tony was eating berries.

_3_ Uncle Bunny pushed Tony.

2. Where did Uncle Bunny find Tony? __near the pond__

3. Tony was on his back because __he had rolled down the hill__

4. Tony looked like a rock because __his head and legs didn't show__

5. Check the answer that shows Uncle Bunny got close to Tony.

____ Uncle Bunny wanted a closer look.

_√_ Uncle Bunny was a whisker's length away.

151 188

Write the words from the story that have these meanings.

1. unhappy _____grumpy_____
   (Par. 1)

2. using together _____sharing_____
   (Par. 1)

3. flower _____blossom_____
   (Par. 2)

Working with Words

A word part that can be said by itself is called a **syllable.** Some words have two consonants between two vowels. These words can be divided between the consonants, as in pic/nic. Write each word below. Then draw a line to divide the word into syllables.

1. almost _____al/most_____

2. blossom _____blos/som_____

3. rubbing _____rub/bing_____

Circle the right word to finish each sentence. Then write the word in the blank.

4. Did you hear the _____knock_____?
   (knew (knock) know)

5. I knew that was the _____wrong_____
   answer. (write (wrong) wrote)

Reading and Thinking

1. Number the sentences to show what happened first, second, third, and last.

   __1__ Uncle Bunny was eating.

   __4__ Uncle Bunny limped away.

   __3__ Mrs. Buzz poked her stinger down on the cane.

   __2__ Mrs. Buzz flew to Uncle Bunny's nose.

2. How did Uncle Bunny fool Mrs. Buzz? _He made her sting his_ _cane and not his nose._

3. Check two sentences that tell how Uncle Bunny and Mrs. Buzz were the same.

   _____ They both got hurt.

   __✓__ They both wanted clover.

   __✓__ They were both grumpy.

Reading and Thinking

1. Check the answer that tells what the story is mostly about.

   _____ Uncle Bunny's wet face

   __✓__ how animals keep safe

   _____ hiding in the weeds

Write the best word to finish each sentence.

2. Please _____think_____ before you answer. (carry, hide, think)

3. We ran _____toward_____ the house in the rain. (toward, over, away)

Look at the picture on this page. Answer these questions about it.

4. Where is Gilda Goldfish hiding?
   _____under the rock_____

5. What is Sunny Sunfish wearing?
   _____Uncle Bunny's glasses_____

Working with Words

The ending **-y** added to a word can mean "full of." The word rainy means "full of rain." Write the meanings for these words. One is done for you.

dirty _full of dirt_

1. grassy _____full of grass_____

2. creamy _____full of cream_____

In rhyming words, only the beginning sound is different. In each sentence, write the word from the box that rhymes with the underlined word.

soap   bright   caught

3. Late at night, the stars are very
   _____bright_____

4. I hope that I can find the
   _____soap_____

5. My mother bought the fish that I
   _____caught_____

Circle the right word to finish each sentence. Write the word in the blank.

6. We played, _____but_____ we lost. (bit, bat (but))

7. Did you find your _____hat_____?
   (hit (hat) hot)

Reading and Thinking

1. Check the answer that tells what the story is mostly about.

   _____ stars falling from the sky

   _____ Uncle Bunny's walk

   __✓__ how Sarah Jean learns about fireflies

2. Why was Sarah Jean afraid? _____
   She thought stars were falling.

3. How is a firefly like a fly? _____
   They both can fly.

Write **R** by the real things. Write **M** by the make-believe things.

4. __M__ Stars fall to the ground.

5. __M__ Fireflies make lightning.

6. __R__ Fireflies are beetles.

Working with Words

Fill in each blank with the right pair of letters to make a word.

ar   er   or

1. Will you read me a st_or_y?

2. We worked with flash c_ar_ds.

3. She took h_er_ book home.

The letter g can stand for the sound of j as in cage and g as in girl. Circle words that have g as in cage. Cross out words that have g as in girl.

(cage)   ~~girl~~

4. ~~glass~~ (large) ~~hungry~~ ~~goose~~

5. (orange) ~~gold~~ ~~tag~~ ~~together~~

Write the compound words from the story that have these meanings.

6. thing of any kind _____anything_____
   (Par. 1)

7. insect that makes light _____firefly_____
   (Par. 2)

In each sentence, circle two words with the same vowel sound as the word in dark print.

8. **soap** Wear your (coat) when you walk down the (road)

9. **grow** I can (throw) the ball (low)

Reading and Thinking

1. Uncle Bunny is Carol Anne's
   _____grandpa or grandfather_____

2. Who jumped first in the contest?
   _____Uncle Bunny_____

Write **T** if the sentence is true. Write **F** if it is not true.

3. __F__ Uncle Bunny didn't think he could win the contest.

4. __T__ Uncle Bunny learned something about himself.

5. __T__ Uncle Bunny keeps his word.

6. What do you think Uncle Bunny and Jumper did after lunch?
   _____(Answers will vary.)_____

   _____

Working with Words

Circle words that have c as in city. Cross out words that have c as in cat.

(city)   ~~cat~~

1. ~~picture~~ ~~uncle~~ (bounce) (nice)

2. ~~popcorn~~ ~~corner~~ (face) ~~out~~

3. (fence) ~~across~~ ~~candle~~ (dance)

An 's at the end of a word may be used to show that something belongs to someone. Change these groups of words using 's.

4. the clover of the rabbit
   the _____rabbit's_____ clover

5. the legs that belong to Jumper
   _____Jumper's_____ legs

6. the lunch of the grasshopper
   the _____grasshopper's_____ lunch

Circle the right word to finish each sentence. Then write the word in the blank.

7. I can't _____think_____ of it.
   (think) thank, tent)

8. She _____bit_____ into the apple.
   (bat (bit) but)

Words that mean the same or nearly the same are **synonyms**. Circle two synonyms in each sentence below.

1. (laughed) and Sonny (chuckled)
2. My (path) is my (road) to the field.

Working with Words

Fill in each blank with the right pair of letters to make a word.

sh   ch

1. Foxes __ch__ased Uncle Bunny.
2. Sarah Jean hid under a bu__sh__.

Write these words. Draw a line to show the two syllables in each word.

3. ladder _____ lad/der
4. corner _____ cor/ner

Add the word part **un-** to these words to finish the sentences below. One is done for you.

friendly fair lock true

The game was _unfair_.

5. The new girl is ____ unfriendly ____.
6. Please ____ unlock ____ the door.
7. The last story is ____ untrue ____.

Reading and Thinking

1. Where did Sonny find Pokey's shell? ____ at the edge of the path

2. Number the sentences to show what happened first, second, third, and last.

   __3__ Pokey appeared.
   __4__ Sonny crawled like Pokey, on one foot.
   __1__ Uncle Bunny stumbled.
   __2__ Uncle Bunny tapped on Pokey's shell.

Write **T** if the sentence is true.
Write **F** if it is not true.

3. __T__ Sonny was surprised that Pokey had just one foot.
4. __T__ Sonny didn't know that Pokey was in his shell.
5. __F__ Pokey is a speedy animal.

163

Knowing the Words

Write the words from the story that have these meanings.

1. broke _____ cracked
   (Par. 3)
2. move up _____ lift
   (Par. 6)

Working with Words

Circle the right word. Write it in the blank.

1. Hold on to the ____ string ____ of the kite. ((string) spring)
2. We planted a ____ tree ____ in the yard. ((tree) free)

3. Say the word *bake*. Listen to the vowel sound of the word. In each word below, circle the two letters that stand for that sound.

   afr(ai)d st(ay) aw(ay) p(ai)nt

The letter *g* can stand for the sound of *j* as in *cage* and *g* as in *girl*. Circle words that have *g* as in *girl*. Cross out words that have *g* as in *cage*.

(girl) ~~cage~~

4. (gift) ~~village~~ (wagon) (bag)
5. ~~danger~~ (grumpy) ~~large~~ (again)
6. (dog) ~~strange~~ ~~orange~~ (game)

Reading and Thinking

1. Why is the story called "Sam Saves the Day"? ____ Sam called Uncle Bunny and planned how to save the babies.

Write **T** if the sentence is true.
Write **F** if it is not true.

2. __F__ Uncle Bunny climbs trees.
3. __T__ Sparrows aren't very strong.
4. What do you think Rosie Robin may do after feeding the babies?

   ____ (Answers will vary.) ____

Knowing the Words

Write the words from the story that have these meanings.

1. someone good at something ____ expert ____
   (Par. 8)
2. wanting to know ____ curious ____
   (Par. 10)

Working with Words

Use these words to make compound words. Then use the compound words to finish each sentence below.

earth birth worm day

1. Come to my ____ birthday ____ party.
2. A bird found an ____ earthworm ____.

An *'s* at the end of a word may be used to show that something belongs to someone. Change these groups of words using *'s*.

3. the secret of Sonny
   ____ Sonny's secret ____
4. the nest of the bird
   ____ the bird's nest ____
5. the branch of the tree
   ____ the tree's branch ____

Reading and Thinking

1. Check the answer that tells what the story is mostly about.
   __✓__ keeping a secret
   ____ a worm
   ____ trouble with Sonny's mouth

2. What did Rosie Robin do to find an earthworm for Sonny?
   ____ pulled a worm out of the ground ____

3. Check the sentence that tells why Sonny was holding his mouth.
   ____ His tooth hurt.
   ____ It was full of carrots.
   __✓__ He was keeping a secret.

4. Why couldn't Sonny share his secret with Uncle Bunny? ____ The secret is about Uncle Bunny. ____

5. Check the sentence that tells why the worm can keep the secret.
   ____ Worms live in the ground.
   ____ Worms have no legs.
   __✓__ Worms cannot talk.

6. What do you think Sonny's secret is? ____ (Answers will vary.) ____

167

Reading and Thinking

1. Number the sentences to show what happened first, second, third, and last.

   __4__ Uncle Bunny's friends cheered, "Happy birthday!"
   __2__ Uncle Bunny saw some strange things happening.
   __3__ Uncle Bunny took a nap.
   __1__ Uncle Bunny decided to eat carrots for breakfast.

2. Write three things that were in Uncle Bunny's birthday cake.

   ____ honey, nuts, carrots ____

Working with Words

Rewrite these words to mean more than one. Remember to change the to *i* before adding **-es**.

1. country _____ countries
2. city _____ cities
3. family _____ families

4. Say the word *keep*. Listen to the vowel sound in the word. In each word below, circle the two letters that stand for that sound.

   f(ee)t (ea)ch s(ee)d d(ee)p

The spelling of some base words is changed before an ending is added. Words such as *happy* must have the *y* changed to *i* before adding an ending. Endings are word parts like **-er, -est,** and **-ed.** Change the *y* to *i* and add the endings to these words. One is done for you.

carry + ed _carried_

5. heavy + est _____ heaviest
6. hurry + ed _____ hurried
7. merry + er _____ merrier
8. hungry + est _____ hungriest